The Man with 17 Names

By Rowdy Gifford

All rights reserved; no part of this publication may be reproduced or transmitted by any means, electronic, photocopying, mechanical, or otherwise, without the prior permission of the author.

Copyright © Rowdy Gifford 2017
Cover photography by Lucy Douberley
Cover art by Kimberly Flack
Edited by Kimberly Flack

FIRST EDITION

This book is dedicated to the women who have put up with me in this life: Lola Berry, my Grandmother; Ruby Gifford Tannahill, my Mother; Marie Parr Tannahill, my first wife; Pam Tyburski Van Sant, my second wife; and Katrina Bauer Gifford, my third wife.

- ROWDY

Introduction

I could be in places where everyone knew I was there but no one knew when I had arrived, when I had left, or even what I was doing there. Most importantly, no one ever knew anything about me except my name was Rowdy. No one knew how old I was or where I was from. My motto was: keep all outward information to a minimum. That way I had very little to remember so fewer chances for mistakes.

Mistakes were deadly.

It worked pretty well since I was investigated, arrested, and let go numerous times. I moved through countries like I belonged and went to federal prison all under assumed fake names. I played by my own rules and those boundaries were what I could or couldn't do physically and mentally. Through constantly pushing myself to the edge in every situation, my ability to survive in against-all-odds circumstances further entrenched me in living by my own rules. After all, I wasn't afraid to die. So every time I lived by the rules I had set, it just reinforced that those rules were the only rules that mattered.

What you're about to read are a few of the experiences I had as what a Miami Judge dubbed me as, "The Man With 17 Names" just prior to giving me my court-ordered, no birth-certificate-verified, social security number-less, name. Who decided that you can only have one name and one identity? Is that one of the rules? Not mine.

I

The Man with 17 Names

I was born in Kansas August 9, 1952. My given name was Larry Dean Gifford. My mother was Ruby Evelyn Berry, Mom was a true country girl. She loved to go barefoot whenever possible even on the flint rock around home. She had auburn hair and lots of freckles, she said the more she was in the sun, the more the sun blessed her with freckles. But she'd never trade time in the sun for less freckles. Her soft smile could melt your heart, but her stern hand was sure to keep you in line.

Bob, my father, was more of a hustler than a worker as I look back now. I didn't really call him dad or father because he wasn't around much. Mom always said he was a silver-tongued devil. He had dark hair and dark eyes and had kids strung all over the country so I have many half-brothers and half-sisters. I think he might have even been married to more than one woman at a time. He could write you a bad check and you take it with a smile because he'd be smiling at you. That seemed to be what put him in prison most of the time.

Before my two younger brothers were born, Bob would often be gone for long periods of time. When he was gone, we would spend most of that time living with my mother's parents. My grandparents had a farm with all types of livestock, poultry, and crops. My grandmother was born in 1901 and was a schoolteacher by the age of 19. That was before she was married to my grandfather though. It wasn't long after beginning teaching that she met my grandfather and they were married and moved to the farm.

Grandma's name was Lola Reed. She was a tall, slender, handsome woman. She always wore a homemade bonnet, could milk a cow, work cattle, and still be a mother and a wife. She was a true frontier woman. My mother and her brother Roy were the only children that lived in their family. Grandma lost a set of twin girls shortly after they were born and then lost another baby boy just after birth as well. Kansas farmland had a way of making people tough one way or another.

Grandma taught me a lot of life's lessons. I will always remember some of the simpler things like how to tie my shoes, how to milk a cow, and what plants and flowers were safe to use for food or medicine. She taught me about springhouses because we didn't have a refrigerator. She taught me how to cure meat, how to work a smokehouse, and how to grow a garden. I spent a lot of time as her shadow doing her chores alongside her when I was too young to do a grown man's work alongside my grandfather. Life's larger lessons like character and some kind of moral code were learned alongside her too. I remember she had great patience; I never saw her really mad. She had a way with all us kids, soft-spoken yet smart as a whip. She'd teach us something without us even realizing that she had. Grandma had plenty of love to go around for all of us.

My grandfather, Ira Berry, was a strong, stocky man. He always wore overalls with a blue, button-up, long-sleeved shirt rolled up to his elbows. He had a farmer's tan with a farmer's work ethic, which I believe rubbed off right on me. He was born in October 1899. He only had a third grade education. By the time he was eight years old he was working on the farm alongside his father almost as equals. So by the time I came along, he knew more and could fix more than most folks could shake a stick at. He taught me a lot of things about farming: how to work cattle, how to rotate crops, how to ride a horse, how to milk a cow, and too many how-to's to list. I seen him work a horseshoe out of a hot forge on an anvil and then shoe the horse he made it for. He was quite the cowboy.

I had two younger brothers: John and Martin. They were six and seven years younger than me. Bob wasn't around much after Martin was born. We lived in a house called the Geyer house. It was a property that was next to my grandparents. They had bought it when the Geyers moved away. It had no running water or electricity. The water had to be carried from a well 500 feet southeast of the house down by the Springhouse. After some time of living there, grandfather paid to have electrical poles put in so we'd have a straight electric run to the house. After that we got a Frigidaire and had the radio playing in the kitchen. We would listen to the "Lone Ranger" and "Hop along Cassidy" all while Mom would do the ironing. Even though we figured we were living the high life then, we only had lights downstairs. The upstairs was still dark and not insulated.

We had a hive of bees that lived on the west side of the house on the second floor. Every winter we would collect the honey. Winter collection can be tricky. You want to make sure you don't bring any bees in the house to thaw out, or they will be mad. Seems no matter how hard we'd try, a few would be hidden somewhere inside the honeycomb. Then everyone in the kitchen would be running around trying not to get stung. It was like a competition of who would strike first: the bee, or us.

We heated the house with wood in a large potbelly stove and had another wood stove for cooking. We would spend the summers cutting and carrying wood so it would be ready for the winter. Since I was the oldest, gathering wood and stacking it at the house was my job. Carrying water to the house from the well by the Springhouse was a chore that fell under my duties also. The well was only around 200 yards southeast of the house, but in the winter with snow on the ground it sometimes seemed more like a mile. Upstairs always got real cold in the winter so we'd have to heat bricks on top the wood stove and put them in a thick wool sock to take upstairs and put them at our feet in bed to keep us warm or else we wouldn't be able to feel our toes by morning.

Like most everything else, bath day was quite a chore and each step really required a list of preliminary steps. First job was to get the water hot. That meant get the woodstove outside burning, which meant make sure there was enough wood already chopped (and hurry up and chop some more if there ain't enough), and get that water carried up and put on top. After the water got hot, we would pour it into the washtub and start with the youngest kid. With each kid change, I added more warm water. I would heat and carry the water in until it was my turn. I always went last – after all – I was the man of the house.

While we were all growing up country style, fall to winter to spring to summer, Bob was in jail somewhere for who knows what. I remember paying him a visit and all I recall is that shortly after that Mom and Bob got a divorce. That must've been the point of the visit I guess. That was the last time I saw him for 35 years.

After the divorce we moved to a place called Soldier, Kansas. It was a small town and we lived on the road that went to the water tower. That meant we got running water in the kitchen, which was a real burden lifted from my chore list. We still didn't have an inside bathroom despite the running water, but I was still counting it as a boon. The most important thing that happened in Soldier was that we lived just up the road from the Tannahill family. Gary Tannahill was a mountain of a man who stood well over 6 feet tall and weighed close to 280 pounds. When he got out of high school the Navy drafted him to play football but had to give him a discharge because they couldn't get his blood pressure down to a healthy level. So he came back to Soldier and lived with his brother and his family just down the road from us. Randall, Gary's brother, had five kids all staggered closely around me and my siblings' ages. Our families became quick friends and it wasn't long before Gary and Mom started dating.

Gary was the head butcher at the IGA grocery store in Holton, Kansas. Us kids all appreciated the situation because we started getting meat to eat at least twice a week, which hadn't happened for quite some time. Mom and Gary ended up falling in love and decided to get married. Another perk of Gary coming along was we now had transportation. We used to have to walk anywhere we wanted to go. But now with Gary in the picture, we could go visit my grandparents 20 miles away pretty regularly.

Mom and Gary got married in Soldier at a small church. Despite the life improvements for our family, I wasn't too thrilled with the wedding so I sat outside on the steps and wouldn't go in. I thought I was the man of the house – I'd done just fine helping Mom with everything for all those years – and now here comes Gary: our new boss. In retrospect I was a pretty hardheaded cuss.

Shortly after they were married, we moved to the south house on Grandma & Grandpa's property. This house was always special to me because that was where I had been Grandma's little helper day in and day out. That house has a long history. Just after my grandparents were married, they moved that whole house with block and tackle and teams of horses over a hill to where it sits today. Old Man Fields, who owned the sawmill in town, helped them move it and had a limp the rest of his life from that job after a pin flew out of a clevis while pulling the house and hit his knee. Nevertheless, the house got moved and still sits where they moved it to to this day. Last time I seen it, it looked a little rough. But what do you expect for 110 years?

I can't leave out my great Aunt Jessie. She was staying at the south house to help cook while everyone was out in the field shocking corn. (Shocking corn is when you cut the cornstalks and tie them together, then stack them in standing piles to let them dry.) Some Indians came by the house one afternoon and tore it all up looking for items they might want. They found a small hope chest and took it along with Jessie down south of the house to a small creek bed where they could break open the chest out of sight. They found nothing of value in the chest. They were so mad that they scalped Aunt Jessie and left her there. When everybody came back from the fields, they went on a frenzied search for Jessie. They finally found her down by the creek with the chest lying beside her and a 3-inch by 3-inch patch of bleeding flesh on top of her head surrounded by the rest of her long tussled walnut brown hair. She always wore a bonnet after that to cover her bald scar. The chest has been passed down through the family from my grandparents to my Mother. I suppose my sister, Betty, has it now: the worthless chest that cost a woman the dignity of a full head of hair.

The south house was also where the first telephone was installed. It was a crank. They were on a six-party line and everyone had their own ring, but if you wanted, you could listen in on anybody's conversation. It was hung high on the wall so none of the kids could get to it.

There was a windmill in the front yard to fill the horse water trough. It also had a hand pump that you could use when the windmill was unhooked. Since we had no running water in the house it was back to my job again to get the water every morning first thing. We had a stainless steel bucket with a dipper for the drinking water and a galvanized bucket for the water to wash dishes and ourselves with. It wasn't until I was a teenager that we got the first bathroom in the house and running water to the kitchen sink. We thought we were living big time then.

The old house came to be known as the Homeplace and it is set on the first 800 acres that the Berry family bought. It might not be anything fancy, but it certainly has seen its share of frontier prairie living from tragedy to triumph and withstood the harshness of time well enough. It has held together from the rigors of daily farm life. In fact, looking back, maybe it's only fitting that I came from such a rough and tumble structure as part of my heritage. But just like that old house, I've weathered enough ordeals, come out standing most of the time, and then just been updated to keep up with the times and still leaning a little to the side, but upright nonetheless. Yes, there's a lot of history in that old house me and my mom and my grandparents came from, and I've remade myself more times than even that house I think. But we're both standing. Don't know how well or for how much longer, but standing we are.

2

First Name Change

There's no way to say it nicely: Gary and I didn't get along very well now that we were both bucking to be the man of the house. I made the hazardous mistake of telling Gary he wasn't my father and to leave me alone. Spouting off my mouth like that brought on regular whippens in an attempt, I suppose, to put me in my place. It was getting to the point where I would be out doing my chores, milking cows or feeding the hogs, and I would see him coming from the house toward the barn. I knew then I was in for a whipping.

To make things easier for us all, I moved in with my grandparents who had moved into the old farm house 100 yards north of the Homeplace. I would still do all my chores for Mom and Gary but I would walk back to my grandparents' house to eat and sleep. The more limited interaction Gary and I had the better things seemed to be.

I was already close to my Grandma Lola from my time as a youngster, but this gave me an opportunity to connect with my Grandfather as a man. I worked with him every day. My grandfather was loud in voice yet never mad at me. He would just talk to me as he was working about what he was doing and why he was doing it. I didn't realize it at the time, but his firm and direct instructions were his teachings for me. He was tough and firm, yet very even handed. Grandfather always seemed to know how to handle everything that came his way. Somehow he turned me into a cowhand. I would ride his horse to count cattle in the back pastures and all the chores that went with it. He taught me to ride, rope, brand, and deal with cattle. You name it, he taught me. I could never list all the skills he taught me to do around the farm and the life skills he set me up for.

We were getting into a decent routine of things when the worst happened. The doctor said Grandpa had cancer: first in his throat and finally in his lungs. He had never smoked or drank alcohol in his entire life. He told me it was probably from all the damn store-bought canned food. He knew he was going to die so he bought Grandma a new light blue Ford Fairlane 1964 four-door. Then he told Gary he wanted us to plant the Evans' place with wheat. We rotated crops and it was time to plant wheat on that particular 20 acres. It was a lot of work managing 80 acres of farmland. In the spring of 1965, we did what he asked. I plowed and disked the ground and planted in early spring. By that time he had already passed.

With my grandfather's passing the rest of the family all moved into the north house with grandma and myself. So I was now back in the house with the rest of the family – including Gary.

By this time, Mom and Gary had two daughters Roberta Marie and Barbara Kay. They were 10 and 11 years younger than me. It sure made Mom happy to have two baby girls. Now we had a house full: Grandma, Mom, Gary, Betty, myself, John, Martin, Bert, and Bobby. The house was full. Turns out that Martin and I had quite the striking resemblance, as most people would get us mixed up – especially since I hadn't been around with the rest of the family for so long. I got more than my fair share of being mistaken for Martin around town.

Something else I got more than my fair share of was toughening up from Gary. The one thing he told me that turned out to be true was that when he was through with me, no one would ever be able to beat me. In fact, the resilience I developed as result of his beatings turned out to be one of my greatest strengths throughout my life. It also forced me to create a part of me that I believe kept me alive when nothing else did. I was forced to learn – despite the crude, appalling manner it was taught in – to separate my mind from my body and retain perfect physical and emotional control. One time I was leaning on the wood fence across the open barn door while milking cows and looking out toward the path. Sure enough, I saw Gary coming toward the barn. I don't ever remember him coming up the hill while I was doing chores for any other reason than to give me a whipping. He got to the point it didn't matter if it was because one of my brothers hadn't finished his chores or didn't do them right or maybe he was just mad. Either way, I would say it was my fault. I knew exactly what Gary's whippens felt like and I never wanted my younger brothers to have to endure such gut-wrenching beatings. It was something I figured I may as well take for them. I was already accustomed to it. No sense dragging them into such pain.

When Gary would come into the barn, he would take a surge milker belt off the hook. A surge milker belt is a belt about 2 ½ inches wide with brass eyelets in it with a bar that hooks underneath the cow to hang a milking machine on. This is where I first learned to separate my mind from my body. He told me that if I would stop crying when he whipped me he would stop whipping me. That was a lie.

When I wasn't getting walloped, I did a lot more on the farm. My time was spent milking cows, bottle feeding newborn calves, and feeding and watering the hogs. Twice a week I rode my horse to the back pasture to count the stock cows. We raised an average of 80 head of Herford stock cattle at a time. Taking inventory on a regular basis was necessary to make sure no one rustled any and that the coyotes didn't get any baby calves. Besides, the ride out there always gave me a good chance to check for any fence that needed to be mended.

There were a few compulsory hours of sitting in a classroom each day too. High School was pretty much a blur. I sometimes look back to realize the only reason I went to school was to play football. My last couple years, I only went to school half a day. I would go home to get the chores done since Gary was becoming very sick by then. He needed a kidney transplant and this was 1968 – maybe early 69 – and all the organ transplant stuff was still pretty new technology. I believe that they only passed me through high school because they knew what was happening at home. You see I never even opened a book the whole time I was in high school. Gary did get a kidney transplant. More than one in fact. I wasn't home when it happened, so I'm not sure of the particulars. But I know it was after I left the house that he received his transplants. He did manage to live to the age of 49 and he did give me two great little sisters. Looking back I wonder if he was giving me those whippens partially because he was in so much pain.

My teenage years also yielded my first name change. This was a legal one at least. I was 16 years old and Gary wanted to officially adopt my brothers and sister. I'm not so sure that he felt as obliged to pass his name on to me, but I guess he figured he couldn't leave me the only one out. The year was 1968. I remember standing in front of the judge's desk and he was telling me because of my age I must sign my own adoption papers. I only signed because the rest of them wanted it to happen. As for John and Martin, they'd never really known any other dad than Gary, so they wanted their name changed to Tannahill. Betty wanted her name changed to Tannahill too. She was more a part of the family than I was by a long stretch. With a few scribbles of ink, I suddenly became Larry Dean Tannahill. My original birth certificate was sealed just like that. Funny how this experience made it easy for me to understand how to change names later when it became essential to my survival and evasion of both authorities and gang-bangers alike.

The highlight – or so I figured – of my high school years was that I met Marie Parr. She was a young pretty city girl and I was a rough-handed country boy. She had light colored hair and eyes that sparkled when she smiled and I was taken aback by her right away. We dated through high school. After graduation, I was 18 and she was 15 so we decided to get married, as that's how I thought it was supposed to be back than. Turns out I wasn't much of a husband. Didn't have any idea what I was really supposed to do. I drank too much and worked too much. I still need to apologize to her for that someday. In a way, I suppose she figured it out because I went and joined the Army and volunteered to go to Vietnam pretty much the first chance I had.

3
Red, White & Blue

I thought I would go and fight with the rest of the guys headed to Vietnam. It seemed like a good idea at the time. I didn't have much else going for me since I didn't know what to do as a husband. Never had anybody show me what a real father or husband looked like, so I figured I was a pretty poor excuse for either. I did my basic training in Missouri. That was an eye-opening experience for this poor little Kansas farm boy. I had never met anybody from New York or Puerto Rico or anywhere else for that matter. Most of the guys in basic were soft and most of them were drafted – not enlisted like myself. Having quite the physical and mental edge on the other enlistees thanks to my rigorous farm upbringing, I excelled in pretty much every part of training. I made squad leader after a week. Boot camp turned out to be easier than working on the farm, and a heck of a lot easier than any whippen I took from Gary.

My AIT (Advanced Individual Training) training was also easy enough to get through. I was trained to be a crew chief on a gunship. Most of it was mechanical training, which came naturally to me. After AIT I went home for one week before shipping off to Vietnam. Nam was where I wanted to be. A whole world and life away right in the middle of the action That's why I joined the Army, so off I went to

Vietnam.

I was stationed in marble Mountain just outside of Danang close to the 15th aerial port. I became one of the 48th attack helicopter company gun platoon. We were called the 48 Jokers. Of course I got the new guy treatment same as all new guys get. I had never smoked pot before, but my first night in Marble Mountain the guys tried to smoke me under the table. My adrenaline was pumping so hard that I never even got stoned. I didn't smoke except for a couple of times after that the rest of the time I was in country. I just wasn't into it. After a short time, I was assigned to a COBRA tail number 092. She was old, but after two weeks she was in the best shape she could be. I had readjusted the pitch on the tail rotor, than retied the safety wire by hand – not with those pliers they give to guys that never worked with wire before. My grandfather had taught me well how to use wire to mend fence. I removed the 6-barreled mini-gun along with the 40 mm chunker to clean and oil them. After remounting them and re-sighting both of them, I sighted the 4 rocket pods on the short stubby wings. Then a good coat of wax and thorough cleaning of the cockpit canopy windshield for better vision finished her off. A good cleaning and a nice coat of wax does make for better speed. With all her fire power and all shined up, she was one mean warhorse.

After being there a little over a month, I was made platoon sergeant of the gun platoon. I'd only been in the Army for less than five months and I got promoted. I think it's because I wanted to be there. I soon started repairing all the weapons, mostly mini-guns, 40mm chunkers, and M60 machine guns, for the platoon and the company we supported. I also sighted in the rocket pods for the COBRAS using the water tower as my target. Our gun platoon became top-notch. Captain Nelson was our platoon leader and also in charge of all the pilots who were warrant officers. The 48 Jokers soon became the ones to call on when needed for a fight.

I remember a time when we needed some heavier fire power so I put a 50-caliber on one of the strongest birds replacing the smaller M60 mini-gun. That still wasn't enough, so I was asked to put up a 20mm cannon on our strongest bird. That took the better part of two days since I had to remove two of the inside rocket pods from the wing to be able to mount the cannon with its under carriage to hold the ammo. I flew the front seat for the test flight. With the belly rack on the bird for the ammo, this made it really heavy when it was fully loaded. It took a while to take flight. Once in flight we were fine: the test fire was amazing. When we were in a dive, the 20mm firing would almost bring us to a stop even if we were in a forward dive.

Whenever I had extra time, I would fly as a gunner on the UH 1H sorties. I would go for troop drop-offs, pickups, recovering mail drops, or whatever it was. I spent a lot of shells with the intention of clearing anything that moved out of the way for troop drops. All I can say is that I was a pretty fair shot for a farm boy who had been hunting since he was a kid.

Since I could fix almost any weapon, keep almost any bird flying, and was a good shot to boot, I got to go on a lot of special missions. Whenever the 48 Jokers were called to do a mission away from Marble Mountain and be gone on temporary duty for a week or two, I was the top-picked crewmember to be taken along.

I flew with the Captain to Saigon to pick up the payroll for our company one time. While in Saigon, he put me up in a presidential hotel. It had a swimming pool with a bar and a restaurant on the twelfth floor. I'd never even seen a hotel that nice before in the real world – my world back home – and here I was in Vietnam! When we got there, a typhoon blew in and we were stuck in Saigon for five days. This place was a lot different than any hooch I'd stayed in at Marble Mountain. I had a full bath with hot and cold water. Saigon was the most modern city I'd seen since I'd been in Vietnam.

While I was in Saigon I had five days to myself. The Captain I flew in with had his own plans. When we arrived, he disappeared and I didn't hear from him until it was time to leave. In my time at the hotel, I met some guys that were in country supposedly working for the US but not in the military. After a day spent talking with them, I thought the line of work they were in was something I might want to get involved with later. This was when I got my first real education on fake names and ID's. The guys kind of took me through the way it worked and also took me to a military ship. They talked me through how to get close enough to someone to lift (or take) the blanks I would need for later. As soon as we were back from the trip, I never saw them again. In the end, we did get the payroll back safe, so mission accomplished. Turns out that mission was very beneficial to my long-term escapades.

One mission I was flying on was taking some VIPs to Camp Eagle. We were flying at an altitude of just over 1500 feet crossing a river when I saw a VC rise up from behind a river barge at about our 2 o'clock position. He threw up his rifle and popped off a burst. I hit my floor mic with my foot and transmitted to the two pilots that we were taking enemy fire at 2 o'clock. At that moment the bird got hit and I opened fire. In that moment, I felt the change come over me that used to happen right before I would black out when Gary was beating me. It felt strangely good. It was like the biggest shot of adrenaline I had felt in some time. I flashed back to the milk barn and knew I was in control. I could feel the power within myself. I became very comfortable with this state of mind and would come to use it a lot in my life. I call it survival mode. When we got to Camp Eagle, everything was fine. We patched a couple of bullet holes with hundred mile an hour tape, but we didn't sustain any major damage and the rest of the mission went off without a hitch.

Another time I was Sergeant of the Guard for the company. It was late night and only moonlight lit up the revetment on the airfield. I was walking the revetment line checking on the guards that were on guard duty for me. I just started to walk to the second line of birds when I stopped for just a few moments. I felt a whiz fly by my ear, and then the bullet hit the revetment wall behind me. The shot had to have been from a sniper of some distance away as I never heard the sound of the rifle shot. That bullet was meant for me and by some instance of sheer chance, I had paused and been spared. I realized in an instant what that whirring had meant. I hit the ground and low crawled around the end of the revetment hoping there would not be a second shot. Since I didn't even hear the shot or see a muscle flash, there was nothing to fire back at. All I could do was drop and get to cover.

Another top mission I was assigned to was when I was flying some VIPs into the old capital city of Wae. I still have no idea who they were, but I remember that was my first time seeing black choppers with no markings. We met them outside the city away from anyone's sight. I was not involved with the meeting; my job was to guard the bird we came in. I had to debrief because I had seen the blackbirds so there was something highly classified going on that I was not read in on.

By this time, I was pretty gung-ho in the Army. I had now been in country around six months. Out of the 30 E-5s in my battalion, I made Battalion soldier of the month. At the final board, the six of us who had been selected that month went in and were questioned on military knowledge from map reading and battle situation decisions, to chain of command protocol and uniform requirements. All six of us were platoon sergeants and when it was over I was selected to be soldier of the month. They put my picture in the Army Newspaper called Stars & Stripes. That's where Richard Lowery saw me. Rich was stationed in country just north of where I was. He went to his commanding officer and asked if he and his crew could come to Marble Mountain and visit me. We had gone to high school together and played on an undefeated senior year football team. I don't remember a lot of his visit as my identity was starting to blur.

I was sharp as a Punji stick with my militant duties, but my personality was really on the fritz. My single interest was in being on or involved in some kind of mission. I felt as though my only purpose was and always would be to be a combat soldier. At this point I no longer thought about anything back in the states: family, friends, wife, their lives, or my life post-war. I wanted to live like this forever: constantly on the edge. Being needed so much in such a high-risk situation. It felt supernatural. Powerful. And it was all consuming. I had lost touch with reality and my identity. On the outside I knew I could manipulate my identity or outward emotion so no one knew anything about me. I went on every mission I could no matter where it took me or what the stakes were. That was my way of dealing with the dual identities I had become. I am not sure at this point if I could tell what was real or what was just in my head.

Thriving off combat, I volunteered for every hot landing zone mission the company had. Since I no longer wanted to go home, I sent a cassette tape home telling everyone I wasn't coming back. I told my wife, Marie, that I was gonna stay and she should go on without me as we would have no life together. My mind was evolving with every mission. With every adrenaline surge I felt my obsession for these door-die missions multiply exponentially. It was the worst kind of drug. And I was the perfect soldier for it. I felt invincible and was so addicted to the stimulation those situations provided that I was completely dumbstruck with what happened next.

It was 4 am and I was wide-awake sitting on the edge of my bunk in my six-man hooch at Marble Mountain. A flare parachute dangled over the top of my bunk, and as I sat looking through it, everything looked cloudy on the other side. I heard someone coming. He walked through the hooch front door, well there was no door, he just walked through the opening and turned right to face me straightaway. He was a runner from operations saying they needed me STAT so I quickly dressed and headed for operations. When I walked into the room they sent me into the mailroom. Ever the good soldier, I followed orders but found that they locked the door on me once I was inside. The Sargent of the Guard was with some lieutenant with medical insignia on his collar who said, "You're going home today Sarge." I told him I wasn't packed and I needed to go back to the hooch to get my stuff. They said, "No problem Sarge. They're packing your stuff right now." And that was that.

Boy was I a wreck. I didn't know what to feel right then. I guess I stepped out over the edge too far and they were going to send me back to the states. I didn't want to leave the platoon behind. Hell, for that matter, I didn't want to leave the country. "Fallen off the edge" – I guess is what they call it when you get like I had gotten. I think what gave me up was my CO must have noticed that even when we were supposed to be taking down time to recover, I just couldn't do it. I needed a constant buzz so much that I would spend my down time in the 10-minute standby hut at the flight line just in case they needed another man to go along. If I wasn't there I would be in the arms room cleaning or repairing weapons that needed it. I was just addicted to soldiering. I suppose that's maybe when I became a part of the subculture of people who live without even realizing what is happening all around them. There was nothing I could do to prevent it. I was powerless at that point to do anything but be sent home.

4
No Longer Welcome

I don't remember much about the trip back to Kansas. My body might have been back stateside but that was all. My mind was still completely in Vietnam. I would go through my daily routine in my head all the time. Count and report, All present and accounted for Sir. That was my first duty every morning when standing formation. Kansas, the Homeplace, the Farm, none of it was home anymore. I tried to go through what I thought you would do when you come home, but I wasn't even really there. I went to see Mom and the rest of the family. That's when I knew I was different. I realized I didn't fit in anymore. I couldn't sleep much or even understand what was going on. Even though I had no idea what PTSD was, I knew that what I was thinking and dreaming about is not what normal people were experiencing.

I was sitting at the kitchen table at the north house long before daylight when Mom came into the room. She looked worried, even uneasy. She made coffee on the stove – no electric pot here. As we sat and drank coffee she started to talk to me. It was mostly small talk, but I knew she was headed somewhere with this conversation.

I could tell she wasn't nervous anymore when she came to the part that she really wanted to tell me. The part that was her whole purpose for coming down to talk to me. The purpose for getting up so early, making the coffee. She wanted me to leave and she was confident that was what needed to be done. I asked her why she wanted me gone so adamantly. She said she was afraid for the girls. At that moment I realized that when your own family is afraid of you, you don't belong there anymore.

Mom was the one to speak to me about it when no one else could or would. Everyone knew I would never hurt or get mad at Mom. We didn't know it at the time, but it would be at least 11 years before we would ever see or speak to each other again.

I had no contact with any of my family for that whole 11 years. I don't remember if I even saw Marie while I was back in Kansas. But I guess she had gone on with her own life like my letters and cassette tape had suggested. That was fine by me because I had married her when she was too young. The whole world was spinning and she needed to have a fair shot of figuring out things without me to deal with on top of it all.

This must have happened about 1972 but I'm not entirely sure of the date.

# 5

The Outsider

As the title of this book states, I've been through 17 names throughout my life. Some I came to live under or revert back to more than others, and I've had to juggle several identities at once while keeping situations and details straight. My life has been on the line more times than I can count. Many times, it was only my ability to keep my lies so fictitiously real in my own head, and yet distinct in front of others, that I survived. Being torn and split into so many self-imposed personalities sure takes it toll on a person. My birth name, Larry Dean, was replaced during my time in Vietnam with a name I grew to identify the most with. It defined me and what I was so perfectly, I'm sure it was the name intended for me all along. It's the name I call myself. I don't miss anything about my birth name or my first adopted name. Neither one have what I would recall as being a part of. Never have I been comfortable wearing either of them, its like I have always been another person. I would have been okay with any name the Judge would have given me as long as Rowdy was my first.

It was back in Vietnam. I had just been out on a very aggressive mission. When I returned I was still rushing from all the adrenaline that was pumping through my veins. When I stepped into my hooch there were a couple of guys I didn't know talking BS to one of my platoon buddies. I didn't like what the two strangers were saying, so I spun the one with the big mouth around to face me and punched his lights out. I proceeded to throw the other guy out the back door of the hooch – and none too gently. I might have put a foot in his ass. When I came back inside, one of the five guys in my squad said, "Man you are one rowdy son of a bitch." Before I knew it, everyone in the company was calling me Rowdy. From then on I've always been called Rowdy.

When I left Mom and my family on the Kansas Farm, I knew the only place for me was back on post in Leonard Wood, Missouri. When I got there, I joined a few guys who were working on a special crew. Even though I was still on active duty on post, I started meeting with some ex-military guys off base. We would meet at a bar that never seemed to draw much attention. It was easier to fly under the radar that way. After hanging around with them for a couple of months, they thought I would be a good asset to their team. I wasn't sure what the team did exactly, but it really didn't matter to me at that point. I just needed something more to do. My duties on base were nothing because so many E-5s had come back that they had no use for any of us. Besides, I needed something to give me that rush of adrenaline again. It had been too long without it and I was driving myself crazier than I already was. My average height, dark hair, dark eyes, and generally nondescript appearance made me a good candidate for their team. The fact that I was strong enough to carry whatever kind of equipment they might need, good at following orders, knew my way around weapons, didn't question their plans, or express any fear about their plans made me the only candidate for their team.

    I believe they knew I was suffering from PTSD even though I didn't, and they knew exactly how to work that to their advantage. When I went to my first meeting to do my first job with them, it turned out to be my initiation. One of the guys punched me in the jaw and tried to knock me down. I was used to taking a beating out of nowhere though and my strong, stocky legs didn't fail me this time either. I took another good punch but he still didn't knock me down. In the next instance, I went into defense mode and I slapped him so hard he hit the ground. That was it. I was in.

    Throughout this time, I was coming to learn that my most valuable skill was that of being a chameleon. My "chameleon" training started even before my enlistment, way back with my step-dad Gary when I was young. I had learned that the best way to stay out of trouble was to try not to be heard or seen. Always keep a low profile. If you're not smart enough to stay clear of trouble, you had better be tough enough to take the punishment that comes to you because of it.

    The next phase of my training came in the army. There I received specialized, intense mental and physical conditioning that allowed me to maneuver in and out of situations without being seen or heard. Since my survival heavily relied on my skill with my weapons, you'd better believe I trained up good on every army weapon available to me. From rifles and pistols to explosives, my honed skillset was flat out deadly. In Saigon I got my first taste of producing my own IDs – a vital part to being a verified chameleon. The army has a way of thickening up your skin to be tough enough to take whatever they throw your way and adapt seamlessly. I prided myself on being that model soldier. I lived for it.

    Little did I know that all of that ruthless training would become the foundation for the rest of my life. People's employment seems to gravitate toward their skills. I had perfected the ability to change identities and fit into whatever situation I found myself in, and then disappear without anybody remembering I had even been there. "Chameleon" was the perfect term for what I had turned into: it was my ideal profession. And it was more than just nonchalance, charisma, and wall-flowerness. I had the weapons proficiency and know-how and tools to produce IDs that would, no matter where I landed, allow me to verify my existence and seamlessly fit in. Even with all that background, I would learn much more from the new crew I was with.

The rough crew I had just been initiated into provided me with a crash course on how to change names and move around the country freely. They showed me how to use the right paper, the right typewriter, and the right information to be able to get driver's licenses, Social Security Cards, and photo IDs, anywhere that you might happen to find yourself. One of the most important things to have at the time was the right type of typewriter printing ball. Most cities, counties, and states were using a certain IBM typewriter in those days with a round ball that spun to the letter that you were typing. That printer ball was exactly what I needed to complete my forged ID production kit. The paper was not as important since you could almost always use a decent photocopy.

After being with the team for a short time, I realized that I was the guy that they were gonna turn in if we ever got caught. I guess they thought they were smarter than I was; after all I was just some dumb country boy. As soon as I realized this, I started making plans on how to get away from them. I still needed some more information from them on how to do Social Security cards and I didn't have the right spinning ball for an IBM typewriter yet to be completely independent.

We went on a shoot-and-run mission to a government building in Missouri one muggy July night in 1973. Shoot-and-run means you leave any kind of ID at home and if you get caught, you shoot behind you and run off as fast as you can, every-man-for-himself-style. I was the guard that night and the higher ups hadn't bothered to let me in on what we were after. My job had been to assemble some fire starting materials in duffle bags prior to the mission. I carried the duffle bags into the building, handed them off to the team, then got to my assigned guard post.

Good luck was shining on me that night. After searching the four upper floors and coming up empty for the target, we made our way into the basement where all the files were kept. We walked into a room that was filled with IBM typewriters. While all the rest of the crewmembers started rifling through cabinets, I got busy nabbing two typewriter balls. I had hit the jackpot. Stuffing them in my pockets, I was ready to scram before we all got caught, killed, or thrown in jail for life. But I couldn't leave the crew without drawing attention to myself, so I just kept standing guard, calculating how I'd get out from these guys and daydreaming about making my own IDs someday real soon. Moments later, one of the guys hollered, "I've got it! Lets go." I still didn't catch what they were after, but whatever it was, they had gotten it and it sure didn't matter to me anymore cause I had found what I needed and we hauled off leaving a blaze behind us.

Some time later, I read about a massive fire that burned up a building in the town we'd been in and the timeline seemed pretty close from what I recall. I had a strong hunch who was responsible for that. It was a serious crime and I'm just glad I was only the muscle on the mission and hadn't been fully briefed on the details. I decided it might be better to start distancing myself from this crew.

I was the outsider of the team. I was pretty sure they would sell me out to save themselves and now they had got themselves lined up for some serious punishment if any evidence was ever traced back to them. I sure as heck didn't want it pinned on me. It would be easy for them to collaborate their story since they were long-time buddies and I was the new guy. Plus, they had planned things and knew all the details. I had merely been the muscle and could easily get blind-sided with a frame. I determined I couldn't afford to wait around much longer. At the very next opportunity, I got my stuff ready to go. Everything I owned fit into one bag and while everybody else was busy doing their own thing, I grabbed my stuff and stashed it where I could pick it up on my way out.

Meanwhile, I carried on with business as usual waiting for the right moment. You couldn't just walk out on these guys in the middle of the night. They had ways of hunting you down if they smelled anything fishy. Silencing a potential compromising threat wasn't even a second thought for them. It was a lot more complicated than just slinking off. If I did get out without their blessing, I would have to make sure I knew where I was going and what I was doing once I got there to keep me off of their far-reaching radar. I was proving my worth to this crew mission by mission – so I was still holding out juvenile hope for a peaceful parting. I knew that everything must be in place for me to make a clean break so I continued to work and wait for the right time.

Although we were tied up in all sorts of illicit missions, there's one that in my opinion overshadows them all and sure set me up for a long time coming. We were to board an aircraft carrier, have no contact with anybody, and I was to stand guard while they took care of whatever it was they were after. Once again I was on the outside. The only thing I knew about the mission was that I was disposable – the guard always is.

Despite the order not to interact with the sailors on board the carrier, I made friends with the clerk who worked in the office where they made the military IDs through some casual conversation. That's what a good guard does – they guard without the infiltratees realizing something is up. My situation was too good to be true. Since I wasn't a part of the main team I had time to move around the ship while the others were meeting. That had given me time to locate this clerk and get close to him. He was proud to show me all around – including his office. While touring his office, he got called out to do something and that was all I needed. In two minutes I had what I wanted. The job had played out similarly to what my Saigon associates had shown me. I walked off that ship with six blank military IDs. This was better than a gold mine in my line of work as it allowed me to move around on any military base in total security. I still can't get over how fantastic that turned out to be!

I had already made a new ID under the name of John Wright. I used this name to rent a place to stash my few belongings and work supplies to keep them out of the team's business. This was my grab and go station. I opened a bank account in Central Florida and rented a safety deposit box where I stored my ID making materials. Back then there wasn't much security on safety deposit boxes so I paid for it for five years in advance. I was worried that if I didn't pay it for a long while out that it might get opened, someone would recognize what was going on, and things could go haywire and put me in quite a bind. This way I knew I would be able to get back to my materials whenever I needed them.

I narrowly dodged a crisis when I was sent on a mission infiltrating a military base called Fort Stewart. My job was to sweep any guard of the building and wait for the rest of the team to arrive. I completed the first phase without too much resistance, but it was sure taking a while for my crew to catch up with me. As I waited in the old, dusty building that smelled like dirt, I heard some type of vehicle coming. I thought that was unusual for the rest of the team to be arriving that way. Sure enough, it wasn't the team. It was the military police. I was busted for breaking and entering on a military base. When they took me to operations, I truthfully told them my name was Larry Tannahill. When they ran that name, my records came back listing me as AWOL.

I didn't get the typical low-grade disciplinary action that goes on your record called an "Article 15." Instead, they slammed me with a much more severe route: I was court martialled! I had been gone so long that I had been dropped from the attendance roll. At the court martial hearing, I was busted one stripe in rank and fined half my pay for three months. Then I was sent to Hunter Army Airfield. The only reason they didn't throw the book at me was because of my outstanding service record in Vietnam. The Judge said letters from Captains, Lt. Colonel, and even a full bird Colonel saying how good a soldier I was got me off easy. The sentence could have been much worse. I should have been thrown in the stockade, so what I got was like a slap on the wrist.

When they shipped me to Hunter Army Airfield they gave me back all my property that was taken when I was arrested. I was lucky they hadn't really searched it. My effects list read: belt, wallet, boots, pants etc. I had hidden my Florida safety deposit box John Wright identification in one of my boots under the insole. That would have been bad if they'd found that and connected the dots.

In all, I figure the army was mad at me for not sticking around long enough to get my official discharge. At that time I was so twisted from the PTSD that I don't remember all of what went down. Nonetheless, I guess the crew I was with wanted rid of me as bad as I had wanted away from them. I reckon it worked out for everybody involved – even the Army got theirs.

6

Is This PTSD?

I landed right back in the military in late 1973. Well now I was convinced that I had been AWOL. At this point it didn't seem to matter. The company I was in was full of sergeants. I reported for roll call every morning and then did nothing all day long. My whole situation really blew. I had no platoon, no weapon, no helicopter to crew, chief, or nothing. I was set in a steel folding chair in the corner of an aircraft hangar and going nuts. The smell of the JP 4 jet fuel and the sound of helicopters on the landing pad made me itch to get back over to Vietnam. I had given my Top (first Sgt.) a request for a transfer back to Vietnam. He tore it up and threw it in the trashcan right in front of me then proceeded to tell me how useless I was. After that, every time I would see Top head my way I would go to the same place I used to go when I would see Gary headed for the barn.

One night I was out drinking with two other soldiers and one of their girlfriends. We were leaving some nightclub in downtown Savannah and heading over to Savannah Beach. The girl had an El Camino so she was driving with her boyfriend sitting up front with her. The other soldier and myself were laying down in the back of the

El Camino on the ride. We were looking up talking about the night sky and stars and all of a sudden we were in a crash. We were on a curve and the girl had collided head-on with another vehicle. The two of us in back were thrown clear out. As I went skidding facedown on the asphalt, my companion went spinning and sliding down in the ditch and off into some swamp. The girl driving was killed. Her boyfriend was thrown through the front windshield but lived. After a couple of weeks in the hospital I got out. I seemed to be covered in road rash and received 50 stitches or so, but I would be all right. I didn't even know the names of the other three people I was with. The girl's funeral happened while I was in the hospital. I didn't go. I didn't even know her. It's crazy sometimes the experiences you can have just by going along with things.

After I had returned to reporting for duty, one day I just decided not to go anymore. Two or three weeks went by and one morning I decided to go back and report. After roll call, Top called me to his office and gave me a load of crap. He threatened me with an article 15 and asked how such a good war soldier could be such a lousy garrison soldier. That's when things went south. Being around him already put me in a fragile mental state what with his history of verbal abuse and my upbringing. I went to my blackout stage – survival mode – just reacting from somewhere. I snapped. I grabbed a little statue off his desk and dove right over the desk and beat the tar out of him. He lost 13 teeth that day and I don't remember doing it. Since then, I've learned that those "blackout" moments are a result of post-traumatic stress disorder. The craziest part is that even now, as I'm reflecting on this instance, it starts to send me back into that mode. I start getting a rush of adrenaline that makes my heart pound, my ears shut, my muscles clench up, and my brain turns off – or maybe it doesn't turn off. Maybe it just focuses in to a very specific zone that makes me feel like I'm on high-alert, like I was seeing everything before through a haze and now it's all sped up and my senses are operating 100 times more acutely – like an animal.

Since Top's office was on the second floor above the aircraft hangar at the very end of the hall, I had to walk past the XO and the CO's offices and all the clerks that worked in the office to get to the door to leave. Even though I had blood on my hands and shirt, no one said a word to me as I walked out the door. I just walked out, got on my motorcycle and rode off. I came back a month or so later to turn myself in. I was sure that they would be hunting for me like an animal by now for what I did to Top. Besides I had nowhere else to go since I'd been cut loose from my previous crew. You can imagine my surprise when I went to the MP station to turn myself in they said they'd never heard of me.

Flabbergasted for sure, I wasn't sure if it was a trick or my head doing funny things, but I never was one to sit around waiting for nothing. I figured that must of meant I was free to go. They said they didn't want me so I left for another week or so and then came back again. By then they had finally pieced things together so when I walked in, they confined me to my barracks until my court martial. They found me guilty, took away more rank and fined me more pay. Then I was sent to Fort Gordon in Georgia, which where they train MPs and have a stockade there. I was under the strictest discipline. I was to be confined to a 24-hour guarded lock down barracks with no privileges.

When I checked in there, I had to see my "boss" -- the First Sergeant over the barracks. Even though I'd been busted down in rank from an E-5 Buck Sergeant to a private first class, Top addressed me as Sarge. He was a tall, slender, country fellow who believed in being respectful – nothing like the last smart-alec, First Sergeant I had thumped. In our first conversation he said, "Sarge I only have one request: don't beat up any first sergeants while you're here." I didn't mind this guy. It was all business. No petty power trips or pride. I told Top I had no problem with that request. After giving my word I was sent to lockup barracks.

Most of the guys assigned to my barracks were in there for dealing or possession of drugs. All had been busted to a rank of private or buck private, so it turned out I was the highest ranking private there. I had nothing in common with any of them, so we didn't have much communication between us. I guess it really pissed them off when they made me Barracks Sergeant. I was in charge of the barracks. I made sure everyone contributed to keeping the barracks clean, beds made, cloths stowed away in their footlocker correctly, and rotated the bathroom duty list. Since they all had authority figure problems anyway, not a single one of my bunkmates were too thrilled to be taking orders from the new guy. I didn't mine though. I didn't care about being anyone's friend and I didn't have anything in common with any of them. None had ever even made it to Vietnam. The majority had been drafted and just wanted out of the army. Quite different from my situation.

Fort Gordon is where they also train the CID (Criminal Investigation Command) boys. They were brought to our barracks on a training exercise. They were all a bunch of smart asses and talked down to us like we were all dummies. They were all trainees with little time in the service and this was just another box to check off their list of climbing the Army chain of command. Since I had seen real action, and given more of myself to "the cause" than any of those mama's boys, I saw their presence and attitude towards me as a real challenge so I figured I'd put them to the test.

There was a fair happening on the base. I could see the lights from the Ferris Wheel from the barracks' upstairs window. I escaped and went to the fair. Since we were in a 6 foot high chain-link fence with razor wire on the top and a 24-hour roaming truck guard that drove around the outside of the fence every hour, it took me some time to find a weak spot to be able to get out. Finally, I found a spot where the fence could be lifted up enough from the bottom that I could slip under it. On my way to the fair I stayed close to the on-base housing barracks. I stole a shirt from someone's clothesline and was happy to conveniently hide my branded "P" on the back of my Prisoner shirt.

I'd been at the fair for a couple hours just lying low but checking things out when I saw the CID boys wandering around. At first I thought they were looking for me so I ducked into a tent and watched through the side flap. They nabbed their targets a few minutes later: a guy selling hash to some other GI.
After they hauled the dealer and GI off, I noticed a subtle change trickling through the crowd. The MPs (Military Police) had started sweeping the fairgrounds holding a photograph of a man wanted and asking people questions. I was sure it was my picture they were passing around. That was my cue to get out! I crept into the dark and headed back to my barracks. On the way back I changed back into my prison shirt and left the stolen one where I'd found it. I didn't want anyone to figure out that it was ever taken or returned. Leaving a trail is for greenies. Getting back in was the easy party. I got back in the same spot I came out.

You should have seen the look on the guard's face when he eventually found me in my bunk. I spent the rest of the night in silence while being questioned and hollered at. When Top came in the next morning, they stopped all the nonsense and he took me in his office.

After talking with me, it was agreed that I would do a couple of things for him and in return, he would ship me to Fort Campbell, Kentucky.

I was given a 15-day timeline to make the transfer. Top asked me to f irst, not make him look bad, and second, not to leave the barracks anymore. Also, he had one problem with a character that he wanted me to throw a beating on as a way of putting him in his place. No problem.

As I was getting ready to leave Fort Gordon, they delivered my back pay that I had accumulated. Minus all the fines, it still left me with a good sum of money.

After reporting at Fort Campbell I'm not too sure how long I actually showed up for roll call. By this time, I was pretty much done with the Army. Instead of reporting in the mornings, I rented a place off base and started dealing drugs down by the river. I knew it was an ironic move. Here I was becoming a drug dealer after how I had disliked all those guys back in the prison barracks. Even at the time I was in the barracks I listened to these guys talk about how they made their money. Between that and what I had seen the guys back in Missouri do with drugs to make extra money, I figured I would give it a try. It seemed like I had a knack for things of that nature, walking on the edge and all rather successfully I might add. Besides, I needed to make some money somehow. Best of all, it gave me that adrenaline rush of being in the crosshairs and cheating the odds. I was based in Clarksville, Tennessee and making runs up to Detroit to pick up the drugs then coming back to sell them. It was a 10-hour trip each way on my motorcycle. I paid cash for it with the back pay I received when I left Ft. Gordon. I would go almost straight north through Kentucky and Ohio. Somewhere along that route, on one of those runs, I just decided not to go back to the Army anymore. If I was dropping out of the Army for good, first thing I needed was a name change.

Luckily, I still had my John Wright ID (the Army was at least real good at giving you your personal belongings back without too much hassle.) I had made enough money and enough connections running the drug line that I was able to find my way back over to the Central Florida bank to empty out the safety deposit box that held my ID making materials. As soon as I left the bank with my felonious goods, I ditched the John Wright ID. It would never be seen again. I typed out a new ID – although I'm not even sure what name I went with. I didn't plan on using it very long, it was just a temporary until I could figure out my master plan a little more and get a better handle on what was next.

Back in Tennessee, I found out that my handsome, ex-army partner had finished selling all the drugs that I had left with him. Time for another run to Detroit.

7
Banditos Motorcycle Club

I bought a 650 Yamaha, all cash, in Clarksville to make the run back and forth to Detroit after my 500 Honda had given out. My Yamaha was a good bike, so I was ready to ride. As I was coming back from Detroit with the usual load I pulled off into a place called Finley, Ohio for fuel and rest. My running partner at the time was Dean. He was of medium build with light brown hair and handsome. That was good as people would notice him much more than plain old me and that made it easier for me to take care of business and not get seen. We had been partners since we'd both gotten out of Ft. Campbell. We were just getting off the highway looking for a place to shake off the ride, but Finley had bigger plans for us that night.

As we were riding down the main street, a motorcycle pulled up behind us. We stopped at a light and the biker pulled up right alongside us flying colors (aka wearing his motorcycle club patch – some people think bikers are gangs, but anybody who knows understands it's a club, not a gang.) He asked us if we wanted to follow him to the place just around the corner where we could stretch our legs. Not wanting to be rude, we rode to the local bar, which was in the basement of a nearby building.

      The building seemed to be as good a place as any to relax for a few hours, so we dismounted our bikes and walked into the bar. It was almost completely filled with patch brothers to the man who had invited us over. When we first went in, we didn't notice that they had hooks on the wall where everyone had hung their colors, but we saw it by and by. Of course Dean and I had patches on also. Only problem is our patch was not the same as theirs and this was their bar. We had a small crew in Tennessee – just a few ex-military guys. We called ourselves The Loners and threw a patch on to make us official. But that night we had come in contact with the Banditos. In the early '70s, they were one of the largest motorcycle clubs in the country with around 3000 one percenters. The 1% is the most worthy, elite, and most organized of all motorcycle clubs. And that night we were in the middle of their den.

      After being at the bar for an hour or so they had tested us about as far as they could go without being physical. I was still pretty fresh out of Vietnam so nothing they did bothered me. It was more like a game. Their idea was to try to get us to back down from the trash talk they were throwing at us. They were threatening to do whatever they wanted to us from ripping off our home-made, hand-sewn Loner patches from our denim jackets to swiping our bikes if they felt like it. They were even talking about kicking the tar out of us if they wanted to. Since we didn't act scared or even worried about any of this, I believe this stunned them. Then we came to the point that they asked us to go to the clubhouse. By this time, all my instincts were on high alert. I was deep in defense mode: somewhere between blackout and survival. I would just keep functioning, but not really go out. My mind was numb to the stupid stuff going on around me. Most were about half lit on booze mixed with uppers or downers or whatever they had. I was just going through motions; keyed up to react with my soldier's training in half a heartbeat. Didn't seem like Dean and I had much of a choice despite it being an "invitation," so we rode our bikes to their clubhouse.

We parked our bikes and walked into the clubhouse – a large old farmhouse-type building on a corner lot in the middle of town. The house itself was like any older house you might step into. With furniture that had been there for a very long time. But that's where the "nice old farm house" look ended, there were motorcycle parts sitting on the kitchen counter along with empty beer bottles all around. The house smelled of stale beer and smoke and motorcycle exhaust plus oil. The entrance was through the kitchen. Glancing around the once-homey kitchen with its large kitchen table by the window and four chairs tucked in around it, an old gas stove, and what looked to be an antique refrigerator, I realized the eight of us large bikers looked rather out of place. We sure filled up that kitchen and the house suddenly felt real small.

The Bandito brother who was dealing with me the most was named Bear. He was expectedly large, sporting long hair, a long beard, and BFFB tattooed on his arm along with a string of other Harley tats. Turns out Bear was a national Sgt. at arms and BFFB stood for Bandito Forever, Forever Bandito.

When we came in the house, they separated Dean and I right away. I was seated at the kitchen table with Bear and they took Dean off into a different part of the clubhouse. I knew that the real face-off was about to begin. Bear hollered over his shoulder to a probate: "Bring the wine!" Bear took two bottles out of the case that the probate fetched and put one bottle in front of me and another in front of him.

Bear looked me in the eye and said, "If I finish my bottle before you finish yours, I'm gonna shove that bottle up your ass." I just looked at him as we opened the bottles knowing it was no empty threat. I took a long pull on mine as he did on his. The wine was terrible. It was called Anny Green Springs. It was cheap and nasty, but drinkable. I downed the first bottle in three pulls and opened another one out of the case. See, my adrenaline was pumping so hard and I had 1000 hits of THC (the active narcotic ingredient in Marijuana) in my vest pocket that Dean and I had both taken some of for the ride back from Detroit. A couple of hours of hard drinking later and I barely had a buzz from the awful wine. Most of the brothers in the house were half-toasted or worse, so I handed out some pills to help them on their way.

The next morning they had a meeting at the clubhouse about Dean and me. What was about to happen was unheard of. We were approved to become full patch brothers. To receive a patch without prospecting or being a probate in the world of 1% -- it just does not happen. They gave me a copy of the rules for the club. The main ones for me were I had to own a motorcycle and have my own means of support. I guess I fit all the criteria at least in their minds. I was now a full patch brother in a brotherhood of 3000 other bikers. What a great place for cover, I thought.

This made it time for another name change though. I had made a new ID in Georgia after picking up the material from the safety deposit box in Florida. At that time I threw away the John Wright ID as I wanted no trail back to the safety deposit box and created Leroy Jones. Now that sounded like a good Georgia name. It worked well. I typed it out in a library and got a driver's license in half a day. But the only name I ever used with the Banditos was Rowdy.

The Leroy Jones name was one that I only wanted to use when

needed. I needed to build a name and background for the ID that would be one I could live as when the time came. It needed to have everything: social security number, family background, the works. Of course the family would all have to be dead and no siblings. And it couldn't be tied up to any questionable activities. Leroy Jones would have to go back on the shelf and I would need a better cover. I had already thought long and hard over the name. It was perfect for me and had a good ring to my ears. I was now William Van Sant. I started using the name right away even though I had no paperwork to back it up. That would come when I got back to Clarksville and picked up my equipment.

    There were times that I would make IDs for certain people to be safe when working with me. One such person was Dean. If we ever got in a tight spot that might come back to him later I thought it was important that he have a fake name to use. But I never made IDs for any of the Banditos or let them know that I had those capabilities. It was something that the less people who knew, the better. It was my survival that I had it for. I didn't even tell Dean where I got his ID I just let him think I had a connection. Covers for the covers for the covers. My life was a pretty complicated mix of layers of lies.

    As in all clubs there are membership dues to be paid monthly. For some reason, I was never asked to pay. I didn't volunteer any money though or ask any questions. I figured they had brought me into this – I certainly hadn't sought them out. I don't think there were any written down records of who you were or where you were at. This was just known within the brotherhood. Texas was the home base for the Banditos and I am sure they didn't want records kept that could be used against them.

    Since I needed to go back to Tennessee with my drug haul

and of course to pick up my belongings, Rock, the national Northeast secretary and treasurer came with me. I think his chaperoning was for two reasons: I was a new brother and they wanted to make sure I was serious about coming back, and secondly I think they wanted to check out where we were coming from and make sure we hadn't been running with an opposing club or something that would cause them grief later. On the trip, Rock, Dean, and I talked about trying to start a Banditos chapter in Clarksville and decided to give it a go. The higher up Banditos were in favor of expansion, so this seemed like a reasonable pursuit.

 Once back in Tennessee, Rock needed a place to stay so we commandeered a trailer that looked like it had been unoccupied for a bit. I had stayed in it before because it was empty but still had the power on. I'm not sure who was more bewildered when the owner showed up: her or us. We were a tough bunch though, so we held our own and ended up staying. The trailer belonged to a couple named Pam and Terry. Pam was a just little bitty blonde thing with a loud, big mouth. She was cute enough though. Terry was her ex-husband and in the Army. When he got out and came looking around for Pam, we made sure he knew we were in charge there now. That's how Pam became a member of the fledgling Banditos club in Tennessee and my girl.

 Shortly after I met Terry, I borrowed his car to make a drug deal. I went to meet some people on a bridge east of Clarksville. It turned out that they were aiming to ambush me and steal the drugs. When I stopped on the bridge and began to get out of the car, they got nervous and started shooting at the car. Needless to say, I shot back and they ran like chickens. I didn't make the deal but was glad enough to escape unscathed from such a jump. I gave Terry back his car with two bullet holes in it. After that I never seen or heard from Terry again.

I guess getting his car shot up scared him enough that between that and Pam being with me he didn't want any part of me. I reckon you could say I was a bit intimidating.

Our Clarksville Banditos chapter was short-lived. I really didn't want to hang around that close to Fort Campbell. I needed to get some space so I could be out-of-sight-out-of-mind secure. Plus, we weren't exactly getting the kind of numbers for our ranks to support a full chapter. The three local boys that used to fly Loner patches with us had turned in their patches and disappeared. Then most of the other guys who came around just wanted to party with us and weren't serious about belonging to anything. We finally gave up and went back north. I moved through Illinois, Indiana, and Ohio pretty freely. A little group of us were traveling around together like a pack. Pam came along with me all the while. This made for better cover you see. I figured by now the Army must have been looking for me. Also I couldn't be sure that the Feds didn't have an eye out for me after all I had been doing. The transient life was my best bet. They might be looking for me, but they weren't looking for a couple, so Pam completed my lifestyle for the time being.

Amidst our moves, we even stayed in Indiana, just outside of Fort Wayne, for a while. I was staying in an old farmhouse outside of town with three Banditos: Corey, national Northeast vice president; Rock, the national Northeast secretary and treasurer; and Bear, the national Northeast Sgt. at arms. I ran with this crew for a few months acting as their muscle. I was pretty much on guard all the time. I always had their backs. I would go with Bear to take care of any type of business he needed to deal with.

One night, Bear and I got stopped on I-75 by a state patrolman. He put us in the back seat of his car saying that Bear matched the description of a murder suspect. He came back to the car and asked us all kinds of silly questions, mainly aimed at Bear, while checking out his description. By now, we figured he was going to call for backup and search us. I prepared for a shake down. I had a 45-caliber pistol in a holster under my vest. Since we weren't handcuffed yet, I slipped it out of the holster and shoved it down into the seat behind me. When the cop came back to the car, he opened the door and told us to get out and for us to get on our way. With my gun in his car, I didn't know what I could do but walk away and leave it there. I often wonder what he thought when he cleaned his car after his shift and found that 45 stuffed down into the seat. I don't know which of us had the better luck that night.

It didn't take me long to get into the thick of things. We had a brother named Cherokee who was a little off his rocker and went out and made a nomad Hells Angels patch. This kind of put everybody in a bind as we had a truce with the Hells Angels in those days. Even though the patch was a fake, we needed to get it from Cherokee and return it to the Angels before too much bad blood was stirred up. There were a lot of meetings between the upper-level guys as we tried to figure out how we could get the patch back without too much trouble and try not to go to war with the Angels. We were already at war with the Pagans and before we could get the patch back, a problem popped up down in Texas.

Froggy and Jesus were riding partners down in Houston. Somehow the Pagans had gotten a hold of Froggy and killed him. They cut his head off and rode by the Banditos clubhouse and threw it inside. Shortly after that, Jesus went around to all the local brothers and said his goodbyes. No one was sure what he was up to. Turns out he built a bomb and went to the Pagans clubhouse and threw it inside. It killed some of them and wounded the rest. He high-tailed it back to our clubhouse and went in the back room and killed himself. He didn't want the Pagans to be able to hunt him down and use that as an excuse to kill more brothers.

Before we could take care of Cherokee, we had to go to a funeral in Houston. Must have been over 2000 of us in Houston. The police gave us a park to stay in and got everyone else out. If we needed to go anyplace we got a police escort. And of course they were trying to take pictures of all of us and people with video cameras were everywhere around the park and at the funeral.

After we made the trip and got back to the Northeast, it was time to take care of the business with Cherokee. A couple of the brothers had been talking to him on the phone and they finally convinced him to meet them at a fast food burger joint. When Bear and I arrived we were to be in one car and Rock and Casper were to be in another. Rock and Casper were going to go in and talk to him and try to get the patch from him while Bear and I stayed out of sight. As they were leaving the burger joint and walking toward Cherokee's car, Cherokee opened the door. I could see him pulling a pistol out of a pocket inside his vest. Casper was standing right beside him and couldn't see what was happening so I jumped out of the car and fired my 12-gauge sawed off shotgun into the sign for the burger joint that was behind and above the car. When things got quiet, no one got killed. Casper got the patch, and Cherokee got the crap scared out of him. We went back to Casper's place to slow things down. We talked about how the story would be told. In those days, no one really cared if a patched biker killed a patched biker as long as no civilians got hurt. We decided to blame the shooting and damaged sign on a rival gang with me as the guilty party. The story checked out enough because people had seen me fire, but nobody knew who I was.

8

Securing A Solid ID

This brings me to Pam. She had been around and I knew her family lived in Florida so I talked to her about going to Florida. Because of the ordeal with Cherokee, I had to disappear in short order. My thought was that no one involved with what had happened knew anything about where Pam's family was, so it should be a safe place to go. She knew nothing of what happened earlier that day, so she said, "Sure! Let's go to Florida." She called her family and got plane tickets. I turned in my patch, dyed my hair black, and headed for Florida. Her folks had no idea who the second plane ticket was for -- I'm guessing they figured Terry was coming along. Surprise, surprise. After arriving in Florida and meeting her family, I needed to come up with a solid ID and a background story for her folks real quick. Her folks owned a plumbing company on Siesta Key and offered me a job. I agreed to take the job but I needed to get a Florida driver's license.

It took me the better part of a month to get all the identification secure. While I was in Finley, Ohio I had picked up a copy of an original Ohio birth certificate. So I filled it out with the name William Van Sant and went and got a Florida driver's license. Next I needed a

Social Security card. We were at a fair and they had a booth that was printing metal Social Security cards for a dollar. So I walked up, gave them a number, they printed me a card and then, just like that, I had a Social Security Card. I used the number to go to work for Joe's plumbing. Pam's dad owned the company. It was a good cover working as a service plumber on the island. No one really knew my name or where I came from, so as time went on, I got more comfortable.

I went to the local Social Security office, told them I had lost my card and handed them my fair souvenir sporting the fake number. When the number came back not belonging to anyone else, so they printed me a new real Social Security card. That gave me a pretty legit driver's license and Social Security card, a good enough birth certificate, and a job. I was secure.

After a year of being securely settled, I bought a motorcycle. It was a custom built chopper from a local shop. Now I had a job, a motorcycle, and the makings of a secure situation. That year I married Pam to make my cover complete. I married her under a fake name and no one in the entire family knew whom I really was or that the feds had been looking for me for at least a couple of years.

Having been born and raised in Sarasota, Pam and her sister Jackie had a large group of friends who they associated with. Now that Pam was back in town, she slipped right back into their company and I came along. That resulted in me getting to know quite a few people in Sarasota and on Siesta Key that year. In the early '70s, everyone knew someone that smoked pot or sold it, usually both. Since I was always looking for a bit of adventure and had money because of my legitimate plumbing employment, I didn't want to pass a good entrepreneurial opportunity. I started to buy and sell small amounts of pot. Of course since I was always looking for that adrenaline rush to keep me on the edge, things just began to get bigger and bigger. The longer you're in the underworld game of selling drugs, the larger your ring of associates gets. In a very short time, I went from buying pounds and selling ounces to buying bales and selling pounds. I even had a closet in an old house that I rented in Sarasota that was filled, wall-to-wall, with garbage bags full of pot.

When you get to the point that you sell enough pot, you get closer to the people that are bringing it into the country. I was to that point. This did two things for me. I got a bulk discount so I could turn over more product with larger profit margins, and it opened up a new market carrying whatever other drugs were in demand at the time. I began selling uppers, downers – you name it, I had it – or could get it. In this environment that some people call "The Underworld," news travels. People soon find out and know who has what they want and in the amounts that they want it.

By the spring of 1974, I was living in a duplex in Bradenton and had hooked up with a few other guys who rode motorcycles. Together, we decided to make up a patch and start up a small club. We would call ourselves the Loners once again. Everything was going along fine: building a few bikes, making deals here and there, and taking advantage of every situation and angle possible.

9
Renegades MC

Before long, the day came when the local motorcycle club called the Renegades came to our house all pissed off that we would start a club in their town. They claimed to have been in Bradenton for over a dozen years. I am not too sure that was true, but at that moment it didn't really matter. After some arguing and agreeing, we were no longer the Loners. We were assimilated into the Renegades. Not everyone wanted to change, so they just gave up their patch and walked away from it all.

I stayed pretty much a nomad not letting any of the new brothers know much about what I did for money. I find it best not to let your bros get involved in your business or get too deeply in debt with you. Worst of all, a lot of the brothers would want in on my action and that was not going to happen. None of them knew what I did to make money, but they knew they wanted a part of whatever it was. The Renegades didn't require too much personal info. I didn't even have to give a name. So I decided it was better to get by with as little as possible. I went by Rowdy and kept my mouth shut about any other details about me. Less collateral damage and risks in general that way.

The club brothers realized I was a Vietnam Veteran and

considered me to be a little on the unstable side. This worked well with my tough demeanor and kept people from trying to always get into my business. I was offered the opportunity to move into the second floor of the clubhouse – a major honor – in the name of helping with the club's security. Our clubhouse was situated in the type of neighborhood that even the police didn't want to patrol at the corner of two streets. This made it easy to defend. Being on the second floor made for a good 360° vantage point. That, with the lack of vegetation around us, made it possible to see any friend or foe coming whether it be from another bike club, or somebody wanting to rob the clubhouse. There were no trees and almost no grass. It was just a square, two-story, faded-white painted building. Defending the clubhouse was any club's number one priority. It was a symbol of how tough, successful, and badass you were.

By this time I was no longer working as a plumber for Pam's Dad. Pam was living with me at the clubhouse and we didn't tell her folks out right where we lived or much about our lifestyle for that matter. I always kept a good relationship with her folks and had respect for them.

One day I saw this van pull up into the back of the clubhouse. I stepped out onto the top of the stairs, which was the only way to get to my place. Out of the van stepped a big black fella I recognized as a guy named Bobby. Two Italian-looking guys, Mike & Snowman, and one skinny black guy, Roger, came with him. What a crew this was. I could tell a couple of them were bikers but the others were just wannabes.

I hollered down to them, "What you want?" They said, "We are looking for Rowdy." Keeping my cool, I asked what they wanted with him. I didn't want to let them know it was me they were looking for without knowing what they were up to. They said they were looking to buy some motorcycles and everyone had told them to stay away from Rowdy, so they figured he was the guy they wanted to meet. After a bit more chatter back-and-forth, I felt ok with the situation and told them who I was and went down to meet them. Bobby and Mike were the two main players and the guys I had pegged as bikers. They had been down to Key West and were headed back to Massachusetts but wanted to buy five motorcycles to go back with them. The catch was: they were leaving the next day for Massachusetts. I asked if they had a trailer, and yes they had a U-Haul. I told them to come by in the late morning on the following day with the trailer. After some haggling, our agreement price was $500 per motorcycle. Of course, these motorcycles were all hot and had been "borrowed" from some other place. As they drove away that day, I'm sure they were wondering if they should come back or not.

When they showed up the next morning, I had five motorcycles parked behind the clubhouse at the bottom of the steps that led up to my place. They paid me and I helped them load the motorcycles into the U-Haul. This accomplished two things: first, it let me know that they were good for the money and did what they said they would do. Secondly, I had just made a connection with the crew in Massachusetts and they were wide open to anything to generate cash. I guess you could say this exchange was grooming me for a long future of "underground life." Before they left, we exchanged contact information and I discovered that they were involved in selling pot. They said they would gladly buy whatever I could deliver.

Even though I'd only been living in Florida a couple of years, I had squeezed in a lot of action. By now it had to have been late summer or early fall of '75. I had moved around enough that I had more than a couple of addresses. So as not to be caught flat-footed, I had made other identifications with driver's licenses and at least one other form of ID. The one I had made out in Bradenton, Florida while I was living in Sarasota was under the name of Sam Smith. There was no way I wanted to chance losing my secure alias, William Van Sant, so Sam Smith was my backup. Always having a backup fake identification was a way of life for me. It also prepared me, more than I could have ever realized, for what I was about to do next.

10

First Run to Massachusetts

A few weeks later, Mike, from the crew I had met up with in Florida, called and said that they were pot dry. They could not find any anywhere with a supply any closer and seemed desperate to know if I had any. So I decided to take the trip up to Massachusetts. I took a white El Dorado Cadillac with a red convertible top and a trunk full of pot and headed to Massachusetts in late November. The Cadillac was a Florida car: it had no heater. When you live in Florida long enough, you forget that winter and cold exist and just how harsh they really are. I didn't think about the heater not working or know how cold the convertible top would get in the dead of winter. So there I was in a white convertible, red top, Florida tags, no heat, driving with a blanket wrapped around me to keep warm, headed to Massachusetts with 240-pounds of pot in the trunk. The car was also an insurance job and would be reported stolen five days after I took possession of it. I did get it through a third-party so I didn't know the owner. The only drawback is when you get a car like that, you're never sure if it's really an insurance job or if it was just stolen outright. Better not to ask too many questions though and just go with it. I figured if all went well I could make Massachusetts in 27 to

32 hours. I wanted to make it without stopping to sleep, just for gas and something to drink.

As I passed North Carolina, it started getting cold. That's when I realized why you'd want a heater that works in a car. As I surveyed the car for something to cover up with and keep warm, I realized all I had was the blanket in the trunk covering the pot. I decided to get it out at the next gas stop.

When you're driving for that long, sometimes things get a little fuzzy because you're so tired. Next thing I knew, I was driving on the Jersey Turnpike. I suddenly realized how ridiculous I looked: like a flashing, neon sign driving unabashedly in one of the hottest smuggling areas in the country. As I drove on, I kept trying to figure out what I could do to blend in with the local traffic a little better. But my driving haze didn't clear and before I knew it, I'd made it into Massachusetts by the late afternoon.

Mike didn't know when I was going to show up. When you're making a run like this, you try to keep everybody's information down to a minimum. You don't want anyone able to say where you are, what you're driving, or when you're getting there just for security reasons. Mike was sure happy to see me and I was more than happy to get there and get out of that car.

Everything went smooth after I got there. Mike paid for all the pot. I dumped the car. Loaded with cash, I was just looking for a good way to get back down south. I found a car service where you could transport cars from one state to another for people who wanted to fly and didn't want to drive their cars. So, I hooked up with a car in Connecticut and drove it to Clearwater, Florida and delivered it. This gave me a new idea for later.

II

The Blue Bus to Michigan

When I got back to Florida, I moved back onto Siesta Key and went back to working for Pam's Dad at Joe's & McGill's Plumbing. Since Pam and I were married, I had to keep a low profile so nobody would know about my lucrative side-jobs. Pam had no interest in how I made my living, she was at home on Siesta Key or the Sarasota area. She had grown up on Siesta Key and I always left her with enough money and pot to keep her happy.

I was riding a rigid frame chopper with a coffin tank painted blue at this time, so when I came across a 30-passenger school bus painted blue, it looked like something I might want. When I went to check it out, it was all set up inside with couches, a table and chairs, a counter, bed, the works. It was all set up for living in and traveling. Even the emergency back door was perfect for putting the plank ramp-up so I could load my bike right up inside.

That was the spring of '76. It was time for a road trip. I took Pam, her cat, and her sister Jackie and three of their closest girlfriends on a vacation up to Michigan. The girls' friends had family there, so I could easily find a place to park the bus. I thought there would be tons of room in the big blue bus, until the girls got everything they wanted on board. Good thing I packed light: three pair blue jean, five black T-shirts, five pair socks, my vest, and my motorcycle. Just the basics.

Before we could leave, I needed to sell some pot for traveling money. It didn't take long to turn a profit. I wanted to take some pot with us so we would have money for the road as we needed it. So the last thing I packed on the bus was a large black garbage bag full of pot.

Before we left on the trip I pulled out the same ID I used to drive the Cadillac to Massachusetts. It was becoming my "on the road name." I was using the name William Van Sant regularly, but since it was my strongest cover, I didn't want to jeopardize it. So for this ride I would be Sam again. None of the girls, not even Pam, ever called me anything but Rowdy. No one knew my real name. I never even considered speaking it let alone letting someone know it. I was just known to all as Rowdy. Also it was important not to let the girls know I could make IDs – they would want one for sure if they knew I had the capabilities.

We took off North headed on Interstate 75. The bus had a governor on it, so the top speed you could get was 55 miles-per-hour. That seemed to be fine as we were not in a hurry in those days. As we drove north, we smoked a lot of pot and picked up every hitchhiker we came across. I had some crystal THC that the girls would sprinkle on my joint when I needed an extra boost. I remember one time looking up in the big mirror that was still there from the bus's school days of hauling kids to see so many guys and girls that I just had to find a truck stop to get them all off. I guess I got that load of people after smoking one of those laced joints. I had driven for hours, just picking people up along the highway. A true act of the '70s.

When we got to Tennessee, we stopped at a pay phone and

called some of my old contacts. We parked the bus in the backyard of an old house that an acquaintance of mine was renting. The house was old and had a large fenced-in backyard with lots of trees and good cover. There was no grass growing in the yard and the house looked like it hadn't been painted in 50 years. There were a couple old junk cars in the back yard with guard dogs sitting on top of the hoods. At least no one would be able to see the bus from the road or from the neighbors. The main reason for the stop, or course, had been to sell some pot.

I only paid $160 a pound for the pot and I was selling it for $325 a pound. I had no problem selling a few pounds right off with the help of one of the guys living in the house. He was pretty non-descript except I remember he had this diamond ring. It was rather large on a slender little band with prongs holding the overly large diamond up. It looked like an engagement ring, but it was so large that the diamond had to be fake. I remember he'd walk around with his ring stuck up in his nose with the diamond part hanging out. In my industry though, you don't ask questions of the weirdoes because you never knew what they were capable of, or if a simple comment would bring some kind of retaliation.

After being there a few days and having sold plenty of pot, we were about to be on or way. Just then, out came diamond ring booger guy. He wanted to trade me his ring for a pound of pot. Since he and my friend had been good help, I decided to keep the relationship good in case we ever needed to stop by again. I traded the pot for the surely fake diamond ring. It made the guy so happy, I knew I must have been taken. Nonetheless, I handed the ring to Pam and she put it on and laughed. She never would wear it as it just looked so fake. She would run the ring up her cat's tail and watch the cat swing his tail to fling it off. So the ring got lost and found many times before it was finally thrown in a jewelry box. The amount of entertainment from that ring and Pam's cat may have been worth it after all.

Back on I-75, we were full-throttle at 55 mph headed to Michigan. The mountain roads we drove through were a blast. We would get buzzed and drive through the mountains and just enjoy the slow ride. After we got north of the mountains, the rest of the ride into Michigan was pretty uneventful.

When we arrived at our stopping place in Michigan, I found a place called East Lake to park the bus at. All the girls would leave to go visit family and friends while I stayed at the bus getting buzzed and shooting my bow and arrows at this big stuffed dog for target practice. People around me in the park probably thought I was nuts. It was a great summer. We spent over a month visiting and traveling before we were back on Siesta Key.

When we returned to Florida, Pam and I decided to buy a house and needed to come up with money for the down payment. Somehow someone talked us into taking the ring to get it appraised. I didn't really want to because I figured I would get laughed out of the place. Boy was I wrong! When the jeweler looked at it and then came back to me with an offer of over $3000 I almost fainted. Turns out it was a 3.85 carat diamond with only one minor flaw. After all the times we lost and found that thing and tried to give it away unsuccessfully. It was the joke diamond around our group. After all that with nobody really wanting it, it turned out to be the down payment for our house. And that poor guy who it had belonged to: he paid me more for that one pound than I have ever been paid for a pound of pot in my entire life.

12

Rent-A-Car

By this time, I had put together enough contacts across the nation that I felt comfortable doing business most anywhere to move and do whatever was needed to make money. I was pretty much open to anything. Of course, it also helped that I always carried a gun, most of the time two. This was just second nature to me so I never thought twice about if I was packing or not – it was just part of getting dressed in the morning. Most people just came to correctly assume that I was always armed. Just like being first to volunteer for all those dangerous missions back in my army time, I was always the first one up when it came to guard the load, protect the load, or collect whatever was owed. Years later, I came to realize that most people were either a little scared or a little worried about crossing me for fear of what I might do.

As I mentioned earlier, when I drove that car from Connecticut to Florida, it opened up a whole new avenue for me to smuggle whatever needed to be moved across the country to whoever needed it. I had to tap into that to settle my own curiosity. Seeing how much I could get away with was just part of who I was. I created yet another name and another driver's license just to deal with this car moving charade. The name wasn't that important, it was just a burner name.

I used the cars to haul drugs up and down the eastern seaboard. When cars were not available, I would find a Rent-A-Car to use.

This was one of those times. I was working out of the house on Siesta Key. But this incident actually started back in Massachusetts. I had gone there to pick up some pot that Mike had gotten a hold of and I was going to use a hot van to move it to New York City. The van was an insurance job for a guy somewhere in South Boston. I needed a transport ride to Florida, so the van seemed like a good solution.

As I started south with the vanload of pot, all was normal. I had never driven into New York City before. As my New York contact was guiding me to his place via the radios we all used back then, all I could think about was how awful the drivers surrounding me were and how much the roads sucked. It seemed like a total irony to me since Florida was filled with New Yorkers always complaining about how awful Florida drivers and our roads are.

Finally, I was able to navigate to my drop-off and trying to figure where and how in the world I was supposed to park amidst the crammed street. The guy saw me and hanging out his upper-story window, started hollering for me to leave the van double parked and come on up. I couldn't help but think that was a real bad move: double-parking a hot van. Oh well, it was his call, I figured. I just wanted to unload the pot, get paid, and get out. So I double-parked, grabbed the suitcase full of pot, and high-tailed it upstairs to a small room on the second floor. The trade-off went quick but I was so nervous about the van that it seemed like it was moving in slow motion. I kept looking out the window to check on the van. The guy wanted me to stay and party but I had to go.

The rest of the trip to Florida was spent thinking about how I was going to offload the van and how I was going to move some material to California from Florida. When I returned to Sarasota, I rented a place on Siesta Key to unload the rest of my pot from the van into. Then it was time to find a place to ditch the van. Around sunset, I found a small car dealership that was pretty much open on all sides. I drove the van right into the back row, left the keys in the ignition, and walked away. Job complete.

In the background of my dealing with the van, I had hatched the beginning of my California plan. I took one of my clean driver's licenses and went to a Rent-A-Car Place at the airport. In those days, you only had to leave a cash deposit. Credit cards were not required. I rented a new four-door sedan for in-state use only. They'd get their car back eventually and would never know the difference of the car having traveled through a few states, right?

I took the car and loaded it with the cargo: pot, pot, and more pot. Then I went to the motel where I had my two pre-arranged drivers staying. The drivers were from Massachusetts and needed money. I had connected with them in the past driving loads here and there up and down the coast. They knew the drill. I gave them some cash and their fake IDs to make the trip. I'd made the IDs from Alabama because Alabama didn't have a picture on their driver's license, so it made it a lot easier for me to replicate. Once they were set and loaded, they didn't wait around long. I think they were gone within the hour.

A couple days later I went to check on the van. It had been moved from just behind the last row of cars and trucks up into the last row. Good sign for me, it meant the car dealer had a plan for it. That tipped me off that the car dealer didn't have a title for the van and didn't care. I figured he must have been a little on the shady side too. A mutual benefit without even knowing each other. Even better for me.

A week later I got the call that the California trip went well.

I said great and asked if they had parked the car where it would be found. They told me no problem, it couldn't be missed. They parked it across the street from the police station. Good work boys.

Some days later, I was sitting on my couch bagging up some pot when I got this hair-stand-up-on-the-back-of-my-neck-feeling. I slid back the curtain and looked to the driveway. An unmarked cop car was parking and a detective was getting out. I turned back to the table that was covered with pot and shoved it into the garbage bag I had just taken it out of a few minutes before. I kicked the bag under the bamboo couch I was sitting on just trying not to sweat too much. There were still some seeds and stuff on the table, so I swiped them off into the carpet. Then came the knocking.

I opened the door and the cop said who he was and which department he was from. He never did ask me who I was, which made me a bit uneasy. I told him to come on in and I walked him past the couch and the table where I had been bagging the pot straight to the dining room table just off the kitchen. He went about telling me the story of a Grandmother who made a living by renting cars, then taking them out of the state to be stripped and sold. He never accused me of anything, he never even asked me anything. He was there to let me know that he knew I was somehow involved. What a ballsy SOB. That made him dangerous in my book! He left without a smile and no handshake.

First thing I did when the ballsy cop left was hop on the phone to my boys in California. "Where did you leave that car?" I hollered. The answer came just like they had told me the first time: "In Sacramento, right across from the police station." Ain't that just like the cops. A hot car sitting there a week already, right under their shields, and no one had even checked it. I yelled right into the phone for them to go break out a damn window, then check it tomorrow.

Sure enough, that was just the thing. Everything worked out fine. The car got towed, I sold all the pot I was bagging when the detective pulled up, and the van got moved to the front row of the dealership. I bought a car from that dealer a little while later in fact, and packed up my stuff from the house and hit the road. No more Rent-A-Cars for a while.

13

Funny Money

Even though Pam and I were married, she very seldom travelled with me. We lived two separate lives, and by now she knew what I was about. She pretty much did whatever she wanted to do and whatever drugs she wanted to have she had. So as far as my illicit activities, she wasn't really a major player. Since Pam's roots were on Siesta Key, I always tried to rent a place close to there so she would be around her friends and family. This way she also had a much more normal life than what she would have had traveling with me. Most of the locals that had grown up with Pam were pot smokers too, so that was Pam's first drug of choice. Seemed I always had plenty of it around. She also liked downers so I made sure to keep those on hand for her fancies as well.

As for myself, the life I lived became normal to me. People who met me would never think that I did anything different than anyone else. Only my inner circle had any idea of any of the things I was doing. Even then they only knew about my dealings with them individually and had no idea of the magnitude of schemes I was central in. Between gigs or when I would need to cool down for a bit, there was always plumbing work that needed to be picked up from Pam's dad. He figured I dealt some pot now and then but never said anything. I was a good plumber and he always seemed glad to have me around. But then it would come time for me to get back out on the edge again and go for that adrenaline rush, so off I would go. Back to the underground life that felt normal to me.

Mike called so I basically went running up to Massachusetts and was hanging out with him and Bobby for a bit. One evening, Bobby sat down and said, "Listen. I got a deal for us and it involves a lot of money." I liked money, so I was keen to find out what the deal was. It started with picking up a load of boxes. Bobby and I went to Boston and filled the back of a pickup with boxes of counterfeit hundred dollar bills. After we got them back to the safe house, Mike and Bobby sold as many of them locally as they possibly could. We bought for 25 cents on the dollar, but after factoring in our overhead, it came out closer to 30 cents on the dollar. To turn a decent enough profit, bills would need to be sold for 40 to 50 cents on the dollar or more if we had an easy mark for a buyer. This didn't count the ones that you could drop along the way. When we were still sitting with way too many on our hands, we decided a road trip to Florida was in order to see what more we could get rid of.

We put a caravan of three cars together: Snowman, Mr. Charisma, Mike, Bobby, and myself. We had two drivers in each vehicle except mine. I seldom wanted anyone with me – it was easier to maintain my anonymity that way and less questions asked meant less stories to keep straight. Being a loner was all around easier in every way. And I never wanted to explain if I needed to be traveling using a different name. It wasn't anybody's business but my own. I never told the people I was working with my name. I was just Rowdy. We were all in a hush-hush business anyway. Too many people in the know can really blow your cover. Most of the boys just thought we were going to Key West to have a good time. It seemed like a good enough cover.

We didn't want to beeline it straight from Mass to Florida in case our fakes were popping up. It would be a pretty predictable route just going straight down the 95, and a dead giveaway and easy collar for the Feds. Instead, we cut across Virginia to Tennessee then into Atlanta to hook up on the 75, which would take us into Florida. I don't remember the highway we took through Virginia, but that was the start of the real run for Florida. Up till that point, we had stayed fairly spread out and only staying in contact via our CB radios. Since there were only a few truckers and us on this stretch of road, we decided to all pull over at the same gas station.

Those of us who knew what we were carrying had had a meeting before we left Massachusetts. We strategized that we wouldn't spend any hot money while we were all together or at any stores on the way south. We made sure our vehicles had good tires and fresh oil changes so we wouldn't have any mechanical problems on the road. We made sure everyone had enough real cash to buy all the gas they would need. The cash was important, because a couple of our drivers were notorious for using hot credit cards. We wanted nothing to do with that while we were on the move. Being off the grid was critical to the success of this run.

We had taken every precaution we could think of. Imagine our surprise when Snowman paid for his gas and spotted a funny hundred-dollar bill in the attendant's register. There was only one guy manning the station and store and Snowman slipped too much info to him. When Snowman saw the phony bill in front, he blurted out, "Look Mike, they have the hundred dollar bills here to!" That was bad. It meant that someone with us was dropping bills along the way. I told everyone to get the heck out of there and as soon as I finished filling my car, I paid real money and got out ASAP. It's just a good thing that back in those days nobody had cameras on their stations and no markers to check hundred dollar bills.

As we hit the highway, I worked my way to the lead as I was going to take them to a spot in Tennessee that I knew we could rest for a while and maybe even offload some of the funny money. When we got to Tennessee, I got the word out to a few of my local contacts and waited for them to show up to cut a deal. We pulled all the vehicles into the barn on my friend's farm property and paid him with what he knew was funny money to be spent after we were long gone. Everyone went into the old farmhouse to talk about the problem of dropping bad bills. The meeting didn't go well. I was pissed off. No one would admit that they had dropped any money for over an hour. After they realized I was not letting anyone out of the house until someone fessed up, it came out that two of them had dropped money on the road. Then to make things worse, one of those knuckleheads had given our host one of the bills when he first got there and he didn't know enough to tell Zero that it was a fake bill. Amateurs. I scared them straight after that and if they didn't follow instructions exactly, there was no telling what would happen to them.

Meanwhile, Zero had gone out for a bit and came back with all kinds of groceries and beer. The town only had one grocery store and one bank. That bill would come back to him and end this, so I knew I had to act fast – and smart.

I went to town to talk to the girl who I knew worked in the bank. A fortunate contact to have in my line. I asked her if she could intercept the store deposit by any chance. She said that that would be impossible because of the way the store deposits were handled. I gave her a gift of some genuine money and asked her to give me a head's up with how much heat was coming my way if she heard anything. Then I went back to the farm to smooth things over with Zero. We walked in the back pasture as I explained what had happened, then gave him a good $500 in hopes that was enough to settle things. With that maybe he could pay the store and hopefully leave my name out of things when the questions came from the Feds. Damage control is sure a lot of work. I still can't believe those knuckleheads couldn't just follow instructions. I guess that's why some people either make it in my line of work, or end up dead or in prison.

We got everyone loaded as quick as we could after my chat with Zero and got the heck out of there. I'm sure we left in a cloud of dust, and by now everyone knew we were hot and on the run. Time wasn't even on our side. We needed to get to Florida and split up as quickly as possible. As we rolled south, no one wanted to spread out because no one wanted to be caught alone.

Leaving Tennessee, I was running drag to keep an eye out for any trouble following us. If it showed up, it was my job to slow them down enough for everyone else to get away. I noticed some Highway Patrol cars acting a little odd. When it got dark, we stopped in a rest area. We all gathered by the van and discussed whether we were being tailed or not. Not five minutes later, with us all still talking, a State Patrol car stopped behind the van and the trooper just looked at us. I think he was checking us out and comparing us to the description he must've had.

We were shocked he hadn't taken us in, or even questioned us. He pulled out and moments after, we decided where we would meet next because we were sure that we'd been caught. We rolled out in stages and the race was on for the Florida line. Little did we know that the Highway Patrol and the State Troopers from two states were only trying to keep us spotted for the Secret Service or the Treasury boys. We were basically just waiting to get caught.

Somehow we all made it to Florida clean. By the time we met at our last rendezvous point, we were all ready to split. Turns out I would never see that group again. I left with the share of funny money I had bought, didn't take any payment or portion of the fronted money to keep my entanglements with the group low-key. Everyone split their own way to Key West, Daytona, and I don't know where else, nor did I want to know. I sure wasn't telling anyone where I was headed.

A few days after I was sure no one was on my trail or had wind of my whereabouts, I started on my plan to move the funny money. I figured the best way was to make a large dope deal. I knew the circuit in the area since I had worked it so much in the past. I needed a player who didn't know me; just someone I could get an introduction too. That came fairly easy enough. There was always someone who wanted to make a deal when they knew it was all cash and large bills. The mark, or group I would make the deal with, were three degrees of contact away from anyone who really had any idea who I was. This way, it wouldn't come back to me.

First thing, I vetted him to make sure he was not a copper, or snitch, for the cops. That was done by having someone else do a deal with him first and waiting. Everything checked out, so it was time to make the deal.

I had to set it up for nighttime so he couldn't get too close a look at the money. I put real bills on the tops and bottoms of each $1000 stack. The exchange went fast, he was nervous. Much more nervous than me – but then again – I was used to keeping a cool head in my "Edge" mode. My alter ego would come out real strong in total control of the situation and I would be all business. Really, my adrenaline was pumping, juicing me more than any upper ever could. Sometimes it would be like I was in a black out but not passed out – just every nerve in my body on high alert. That was The Edge. And like any drug, I would look forward to when I would cross over that threshold. The poor nervous guy getting the bills was sure intimidated by me in my Edge mode. My reputation had preceded me. His connections checked out, and he really just wanted to make the deal and scram. He found out he was burned soon enough after the deal. Two days later, the story was flashed all over the local TV news and across the papers was, "Do not accept these $100 bills." The money had been printed with only six different serial numbers. All six were plastered on the TV screen. They had dumped lots of them in nightclubs and strip joints.

    I knew the heat was going to be coming I had just hoped it wouldn't be so fast. I started selling the cocaine I had bought from him for lowball prices the next morning. I had to get rid of it before he tried tracking me down and taking it back. Luckily, it flew for such a deal so all I had left to do was trade in my car, grab a different ID, swing by the courthouse to pick up new vehicle tags, and get out of Florida. All in a day's work.

    I was through with funny money forever after that. There were just too many people involved, too many liabilities and variables beyond my total control, and way too many Feds chasing that money!

14

Motor City Madness

I had to get out of Florida for a while to let the heat cool off. I rented a U-Haul truck and decided to take a run to Detroit. I used a different ID to set up the rental and to drive the truck in case of problems. There was actually a lot of organization and mental planning to keep my IDs straight. You had to make sure certain scenarios matched up, didn't cross, and that things always checked out. It took a lot of work and I don't think a normal person could have kept it all straight. One of the problems with changing names is having the ability to remember all the right numbers. If you jumble your numbers, you're as good as caught. You start with the date of birth. Then it's social security, driver's license number, and house address. After the numbers comes background. Place of birth first, always an only child with parents both deceased. That's just the easy part of it to get started. From there you must be able to remember and repeat that without fail, falter, or hesitation under any amount of pressure normally and calmly. I would spend hours by myself going over these items until I was sure I could do it. You can't be nervous. It must be natural – like real life.

For this go-round, I was taking Pam, her sister Jackie, and my German Shepherd dog Sam. I put all kinds of junk in the back of the truck: old dressers, boxes, a TV, and other random stuff to hide the three very large garbage bags bulging with pot.

I had procured the pot from a connection I had in central Florida. My connection was bringing the pot in through Mexico. It was actually a good, Colombian gold-type of pot that was very popular and very expensive at that time. My plan was to sell the pot in Detroit to continue my money flow so we could do whatever it was that we wanted to do next.

The trip up to Detroit was pretty uneventful. It heated up a little bit here and there once we arrived. For example, shortly after we first got there, while we were in some urban park waiting for a deal to go down, a cop car pulled up and asked us a few questions. I guess little Jackie got pretty nervous because she took a pistol I kept in the glove box and stuffed it in her waistband, covering it with her shirt. Of course she was trying to be secretive about it, but the cop knew exactly what she'd done. He took it from her without much struggle and suddenly they start running names and all that and find she's a minor traveling with her sister and her sister's husband. Thankfully they only checked out Jackie's ID, but Pam and me were still caught cause now they were taking Jackie to the juvenile hall and contacting her parents. I knew that her parents would be upset when they were contacted, but her father also knew that I always took good care of his daughters so now wasn't the time to worry about that. I would work that out a bit later.

While all this was processing, the cops asked a lot of questions and looked at everything in the truck. Since my dog, Sam, was in the front seat of the truck, they didn't want anything to do with the cab. But they had no reservations about poking around in back. They had me open the door on the back of the truck and start opening black garbage bags to check inside. I had prepared for just this situation though, so had no qualms starting with the first few bags. After the first six or seven of the 20 bags turned up smelly dirty clothes, random household goods, and a bunch of other junk I had thrown in, the cops got bored and decided it wasn't going anywhere. They told me I could stop, which was quite a relief. I had figured right: I could outsmart the cops pretty much every time. It just took some intuitive planning combined with putting on my Midwest act of total compliance, nothing-to-hide charisma.

We still had Jackie to sort out though. The cops took her off to juvenile hall and kept the pistol for themselves. It was a chrome-plated .38, a real nice piece. What a shame –I hated to lose it. But gone it was. There wasn't anymore time to bemoan that fact. I had a lot on my plate to figure out and needed to figure it out fast. I had to come up with a plan to spring Jackie, sell our pot, and get out of Detroit.

I connected with a single buyer for the load of pot, which was preferred instead of piecing it out all night and having to go all over. The fewer transactions the better. Plus, the day was passing fast. We had our incident with the cops around 10 am that morning and now it was almost 5 pm. It was time to find juvenile hall and see what we could do about Jackie.

We didn't know the address for Juvy and without the convenience of the Internet back then, our only shot was to find a phone book. It took a good hour to find a book that was intact, but we finally had our heading.

When we arrived at the hall, Pam went in since she was family and only direct relatives were allowed to enter. Little Jackie had never been in trouble before in her life, so I knew she must be scared to death. Jackie was only about 17 at the time so she was still under age, which turned out for the best. Pam learned that the hall had already called Jackie's parents and gave them the story. Her folks had already sent airfare to them to send her home. Luckily, Pam hit it off with the head lady at the hall who gave her permission to come see Jackie around 11 that night.

We came back just after 11. I sent Pam in with a hundred dollar bill in her pocket. In the '70s a hundred dollars went a long way. Long enough, in fact, to get a kid handed over to us in just 20 minutes. Pam and Jackie came bouncing right out the front door of Juvy Hall. Relief washed over us all and we wasted no time leaving Detroit. I had Jackie call her Mom and Dad as soon as we were out of town a bit to let them know everything was okay. I am sure that her parents were having second thoughts about letting little Jackie come on this trip but not a word was ever said. I really don't know if they ever got their money back for the ticket they bought, and they never said anything about sending her straight home. They were mostly just glad she was okay and that things got straightened out. To be totally honest I am not sure they believed that it really happened. They never said, so I guess we will never know.

Of course by this time, Pam and Jackie both knew what I did for a living with my selling pot and all to make money. I kept them in the dark though about all my name changes, identities, and other activities that I was involved in. This was the '70s and nobody thought anything about pot. It was standard fare as far as most folks were concerned. Just part of life. This Detroit incident was one of the few times that Pam was involved to try to help me get out of a problem that had arose from my type of lifestyle. I always tried to keep her involvement to a minimum, and this situation made me recommit to keeping it that way. I didn't want to pull her into my "underworld" life. Maybe it was a strange philosophy to hang on to in my line of work, and I don't know if I picked it up more from my farm-boy roots and grandparents' old-fashioned values or from my dedicated service in the Army, or if it was just who I am, but I always felt that I was supposed to take good care of those I chose to be with me in my life. That translates to: Don't put them in harm's way in spite of whatever lifestyle I choose to live. This wasn't always possible, but it was always at the forefront of my mind. This whole experience was a strong reminder of just that. Enemies, cops, Feds, Bounty Hunters – they could do whatever they wanted to me without it fazing me too much. But this was one of the few things that could affect me: what people close to me went through because of my lifestyle.

The trip back to Florida went well. The trip had taken a bit over three weeks, so that was enough time for the heat to have turned to some other direction. The one good thing about large cities is they have enough going on that things can become "cold cases quick." Having my adrenaline needs met and a wake up call with putting my loved ones on that Edge with me and them not knowing how to handle it like I had trained myself to, I was ready to freeze for a bit. I returned the U-Haul without any questions as to why a local rental had accumulated so many miles. Pam and Jackie talked things out with their folks, and it all turned out well. No one got hurt. Their parents weren't even mad at me at all. I don't know what story they told their folks but it worked for me.

15

Renegade National

It was time to slow things down a little bit. I had been involved in so much lately that it was time to just sit back and lay low. That was the hard part for me: laying low. I missed the adrenaline buzz I got from living on the edge. But lying low was important to keeping your options open when you had the kind of tag on you that I had. I suppose most people wouldn't think hanging around with a motorcycle club would be laying low. But for me it was! It's not like I fit in anywhere at this time so being in the club had a way of keeping most people away from me. In those days people had a healthy fear of motorcycle clubs.

It felt good to be back hanging with my Renegade brothers. But since I can't sit still, it wasn't long before I was itching to get involved with something else. This next venture seemed harmless enough. The man who first organized the club was from the small town of Sparta, Tennessee. My patch brothers Roach and Zero and I decided to go up to Sparta and start up a chapter of Renegades there again.

Roach was like a son to me. I had met him when he was only 16 years old. He didn't have a Father, at least not one that he'd ever known, and he ran pretty wild on his own. He was a tall, slender youngster with plenty of energy eager to prove his metal amongst our club. He had been with me when the Renegades turned us from Loners to Renegades. He also lived with Pam and I for quite some time before that. He was quiet like me and respectful yet ready to prove himself to me and everyone else. I seen that he had been watching and learning while being around me. He would always keep his leftover butts of smoked joints, called roaches, so everybody just called him Roach.

By this time, Roach was a full-grown man who had filled out to be a pretty stout fellow. His swarthy complexion gave him away as half Indian, and his long obsidian hair accented that even more.

Zero was originally from Sparta, Tennessee too like the founder of the Renegades. He still had sisters who lived there, but I never was too sure about the whereabouts of his folks. He was shorter than me with long blonde hair, a little stocky, and always had a great attitude. Nothing seemed to bother him. I believe that's how he got the nickname Zero: his opinion of anything was zero. And that caused zero drama and zero problems for him for the most part.

Anyway, the three of us decided to ride our bikes north to Sparta. Roach was riding a sportster, Zero was riding a pan head chopper, and I was riding a '68 shovel-pan chopper. It was dark as we were riding the beltway around Atlanta, GA when the headlight on Zero's pan died out. We needed gas anyway, so we stopped at a station and tried to fix the headlight at the same time. We were flying colors, which means we were wearing our Renegade patches, and as we stopped at the gas station, a Highway Patrol car and an Atlanta cop pulled in behind us. They didn't ask us for identification, they just wanted to know if we had came for the Outlaw National going on in downtown Atlanta. It was a mandatory meeting for all members of the Outlaws' motorcycle club but we knew nothing about it and told them so. We explained that we were just stopping to fix the light and fuel up and then we'd be on our way. I guess those cops were eager to get rid of us because the next question they threw at us was, "Well can't you ride it without the headlight working?" Of course we said yes because we were all carrying guns and pot and didn't want them to be mad at us or search us. So we fueled up and I changed bikes with Zero since I figured I could handle the headlight-less bike as long as they led the way. This was close to midnight and although the beltway had staggered streetlights, the roads north of that heading into Tennessee were all pitch dark. It was quite the night ride.

We rode on through the night with a couple more rest stops for gas and pulled into Sparta just after daylight. From there, we went to Zero's old farmhouse that was somehow tied to his family. We parked our bikes in the yard, went inside to drink a couple of beers, and sat around relaxing to get the road off of us until we fell asleep.

We'd been in town for a month or so and I had been busy making connections with some of the local wheelers and dealers. It came time for us to make another road trip to the Renegade National. We decided to have a goodbye party before we left, so we rode our bikes to the lake down south of town. Roach, Zero, I and I don't remember who else all rode our bikes out, but there was a good-sized crowd of us. We were all pumped up about an upcoming national run to Virginia. We had made sure all the bikes were ready to go and it was time for a pre-party party.

While at the lake someone got me to eat a 750 plasidyl, commonly called a "Mean Green." This is a strong downer that we had a bunch of and everybody was passing them around. I don't remember who it was or why I ate it because I knew I couldn't handle downers.

That was a sign things were not going right. The next sign was that they got me to ride a sportster back into town instead of one of the choppers -- which when I was in my right mind, I would never have done. Sportsters just weren't my thing. But that's just how it worked out. We came off of the gravel lake road onto the newly paved asphalt road and headed toward town. I was wobbling pretty good and eased off to the side of the road. After a few minutes, I decided I'd better get going or I'd never make it back. As I merged back onto the asphalt from the shoulder, I didn't see the 3 inch rise between the medium and the asphalt.

When I hit the hump, I lost all control and landed on my back sliding across the road. I flew backwards into the pan head's right front foot peg, which was a railroad-spike-type of foot peg. It went clear through the back of my metal Prussian helmet and shook me damn good. Everything got real fuzzy after that. Zero ran over me with the front end of the other chopper, and then everything came to a stop. It had all just happened in just a few seconds.

I woke up in the hospital with the doctor saying I had shaken my brain loose from my skull. He prescribed a week or two in bed and then maybe I would come out okay. Well I knew we had a national run coming up, so there was no way I could just lay there and miss that. National runs are mandatory – everyone has to be there. If you don't show, you get yourself into a whole lot of trouble. So I told the doc thanks but I got to go. I put my clothes on and with the help of Roach and Zero I left the hospital.

Things kind of jumped around in my head after that. Next thing I remember I was leaving Sparta in the back of a medium sized U-Haul truck with some bikes, a couple of sleeping bags, and a few duffel bags of gear alongside me. All I remember of the trip to Virginia was that every time they stopped for gas, the door would roll up to make sure I was still alive.

We reached the Virginia National and everybody was relieved to find me alive when they opened up the back truck door for the last time. They took me out and walked me into some old, abandoned farmhouse where the national was being held. They laid me out on a sleeping bag and had the brothers' old ladies keep an eye on me. I slept through the whole national. I didn't make any of the meetings, I don't remember eating or drinking anything. That turned out to be the last national run I made as a Renegade.

I finally started to come back around on the trip back to Tennessee. When they stopped for gas at least I could get out of the truck and walk around or eat something. The closer we got to Sparta, the stronger I got. I was even able to ride one of the bikes the last 25 miles back into town. I clearly remember being so glad to be back in the wind again. Riding has always been a time to clear my mind and it sure felt good that day.

Well so much for the big mandatory national run. I made it to it and back and don't know anything about what happened while I was there. Was it worth it? Since I can't remember much, I'm not really sure.

16

The Sheriff & the Spencer Mountain Boys

Since Sparta was a small town, the Renegades being there made the local Sheriff pretty mad. He really had a dislike for me as he figured I was the " ring leader" and sooner or later would cause him some type of problems. Since I made it a point to never have to show my ID to anyone, he could only go by what he could find out from snitches who might have talked to someone close to me. I'd always just used the name Rowdy and like anybody who'd ever tried, he sure couldn't dig much up under that name. Roach was one of the few who would have known that I had more than one ID, but he didn't know what it might be or even which one might be my original. He never would have blown my cover.

The Sheriff felt that biker groups were never known to promote the wholesome well being of a community, and we were no exception. He especially didn't like me. He felt I was causing too much of a change in the locals. He wanted me gone and didn't mind making it obvious.

On the main drag in town, there was a small 24-hour diner right across from an ice cream place that looked like a Dairy Queen. It was the local late night hangout place for our late-night crew.

I was there having coffee one night when across the street at the ice cream place, a car parked facing the diner head-on. Someone walked in and hollered at me, "Those guys across the street are looking for you." I figured I'd better go deal with whoever was calling me out. As soon as I stepped outside, the driver's door opened and this guy got out with a shotgun. I saw him begin to draw down on me over the car door, so I started running at him full speed. Just as he was ready to fire, I drop kicked the car door into him. The shotgun went off up in the air and without missing a beat, I swung around the car door and grabbed the gun right out of his hands. What was that SOB thinking? I didn't give him a chance to explain, I just started to pound the crap out of him.

As this was going down, one of the local boys who had been with me in the diner had run over to back me up and was wailing on the passenger in the car. When their pounding was winding down, the cops showed up. They told the two guys who had come to shoot me something, and then sent them on their way. The cop told the local boy who helped me to go on about his business. Then the cop turned to me and asked me if I would come along with him to the courthouse to file charges. I declined – better to keep out of the system no matter what side you're on, cause eventually it would turn out that I was on the wrong side. So he asked if I would bring the shotgun down to the Sheriff's office and I agreed.

When I got to the Sheriff's office, the Sheriff was sitting there like he was waiting for me. I thought that was odd since it was the middle of the night. The other weird thing was that the two guys who had just tried to shoot me were there in his office too. When I handed the shotgun to the Sheriff, he handed it to back to the guy who tried to shoot me. Then he said to them, "I thought you Spencer Mountain boys were supposed to be the best, but you can't even take care of one mangy biker. Now get out of here."

They scrambled out, leaving just me and the Sheriff staring each other down, not saying a word. So now I knew he had put a hit out on me and he was waiting to see what I might do about it. I kept my head held high and my jaw stiff and left his office without saying a word.

17

Kicked Out

After recovering from that run-in, I needed to get back to work making some money. While being in town, I had met a man by the nickname of Gerber. As you might guess, he was a Gerber-baby look-alike, except that his baby-face and thinly combed baby hair were sitting on top of a muscular, 250-pounds of grown man. He was the local pill dealer and he specialized in downers. Since pot was hard to come by in a lot of places in the country, the business had turned to pills. Small pill packages were a lot easier to move than bails or even pounds of pot. A lot of people in those areas didn't even smoke pot, so drug dealing economics 101: to make money you deal with the product at hand. I bought 10 bottles of 100-count seconals (we usually just called them REDS) from him and made plans to go to Florida to turn a profit.

I bought a second-hand car from the local Chevy dealer and was out of Tennessee before long. I had no problem selling all the REDS in Florida and made a decent profit while doing so. It also happened to be the third Monday of the month, which meant it was the mandatory Renegades meeting at the clubhouse. I figured I should show up since I was there anyway.

I got to the clubhouse at 7:30 pm without thinking much of it. It was just business as normal – stopping by the clubhouse – my local chapter clubhouse. But when I tried to walk in, the guys wouldn't let me. They made me wait on the porch and I couldn't figure out if what was going down was going to turn out good or bad. When the Enforcer finally came out and permitted me to come into the meeting, I was told to leave my two guns with the guard at the door. Now I knew I was in for a bad meeting. Since I wasn't the one calling the shots though, I complied. Once I got in, there wasn't a whole lot of conversation. In fact, it seemed strangely hushed. They got down to business pretty quick though and the bottom line of the meeting was that they were throwing me out of the Renegades "for the betterment of the club." I had never heard of anyone being thrown out of a motorcycle club for the betterment of the club. I knew darn well it was because I wouldn't let them in on my business. But there it was and that's how it was. I turned in my Renegades patch, walked out to the porch, collected my two pistols, and drove away. It wasn't like any of them were friends or for that matter even liked me. I believe they were more worried about how I might react considering they thought me a bit unstable. Fear has a way of keeping people a safe distance from you.

As time passed, I found out more of the underlying reasons why they felt like they had to exorcize me from some of the club brothers who were still on good terms with me. I guess I was just too much of a nomad to be in "their" club. Plus I was good at keeping my business to myself and not open with them about it pissed them off pretty good. It was just as well for me because I didn't like taking orders from anybody, and most of them were just blowhards. They only acted tough and did foolish things when they were in a crowd with their other brothers around.

Now that we had cut ties, it made absolutely no difference to me. I went on about my business. Since I had left I had nothing tying me down and Gerber had sent word that he wanted to talk to me about a little business proposition.

18

The "Little" Safe

When I returned Gerber's message, he told me he knew about a safe that had a sweet payload inside. He had been renting from a slumlord who made all his renters pay with cash. He'd been renting from this man for over a year and finally had been to the place where the man lived. On two occasions when Gerber had paid his rent, the landlord's safe was open, and he was able to see stacks and stacks of cash inside.

Gerber was lining up a hit on the safe, but he needed my brains to organize the heist and provide some muscle. He wanted to know if I could get a team together, plan it out, and then we'd split the money evenly. I told him I'd run a set up, check it out, and let him know. I spoke to the best safe man I knew up in Massachusetts. His name was Bobby. Bobby was a beastly black man standing over 6 feet tall and weighing about 250 pounds of solid muscle. Bobby and I got along really well because we both liked living on the edge a little bit. I told Bobby I had cased the house and worked out a plan to get in and out. We talked about doing the job around the fifth of the month so that way everyone would have just paid the rent. He was in. I went back to settle the details with Gerber.

When I got back to Tennessee to collaborate with Gerber, he had already been working on a different angle. I told him about Bobby and that he wanted an equal share: we would split the loot in thirds. Turns out Gerber didn't like that, so he weighed in with his own fix. Gerber had already felt out a few local guys who were willing to take a much smaller payment. Gerber wanted to just use them as muscle to get the safe out of the house and then work on cracking it at his leisure. Bobby and me had wanted to do the opposite: get in, crack it, wipe it out, and then scram all on the same night. Gerber played the veto card, but he still wanted me as his right-hand man. Too eager for a payout and craving action, I agreed even though I was skeptical of Gerber's plan.

Our team met up to finalize the plan details: I would open the door and the three local guys would go in with me. We'd bring the safe outside and set it down onto the driveway. A truck would be parked across the street and I would give Gerber a signal with a flashlight to back in and we would lift the safe into the back of the truck, Gerber's guys would jump in to hold it securely, and I would bolt while Gerber sped off.

That was the way it was supposed to go down. Now this is how it actually went down.

We picked the night a fair was in town and watched the house to make sure the landlord and his cronies were gone. As soon as the house was empty, we got to work. I had parked my car in the gas station just around the corner from the safe house. Gerber parked his truck in the alley directly across the street from the driveway of our target house and waited for the three short flashlight bursts.

So the four of us walk right up to the house. As I'm picking the lock on the back door, I hear a window crash and someone hollering. I rushed to the back of the house to find one of Gerber's dumb asses had used a tire iron to break a window. Except when he hit the window, he hit it so hard it went through the window and he had cut his arm real bad. As soon as he cut his arm, he freaked out and threw the tire iron somewhere out in the yard while bleeding all over the place. We should've called it a night right then but we didn't. After a stunt like that, we should have realized we weren't getting anywhere with the quality of help Gerber had solicited. But now that the window was broken, the landlord would only increase his security measures, so this was for sure the last chance we'd have at the safe.

We all returned to the back door and I quickly picked the lock to get in. The safe was behind a bi-fold door in the office was by the house's back door. When I parted the bi-fold door uncovering the safe, there stood a huge, 800-pound safe. So much for a "little" safe! Gerber hadn't indicated that it was going to be nearly that massive. To move the safe we would have to tip it over, push it across the floor to the back door, then finesse it down five steps to the sidewalk and out onto the driveway. I was pissed, but not one to give up, I adapted mentality and got to work leading the other guys.

First thing I had to do was get our team back together. We needed every pound of muscle available to make this work. One guy was running all around the house looking for stuff to steal. I cussed at him to get over here and do his job. We finally got the safe to the door. It took us much longer than I had hoped. When we got it out onto the stoop, the five concrete steps seemed impossible. We just shoved with everything we had and let her go. Down she crashed; her iron edge breaking through the concrete and embedding herself in the sidewalk. We still had 10 feet of sidewalk to push it across after we rolled it out of the whole it had punched in the sidewalk at the bottom of the stairs. When we finally got it to the driveway, I signaled Gerber to back in. Of all the idiot criminals, Gerber proved his place at the top with his next move. The dummy pulled the truck in forwards instead of backwards.

So now, all five of us had to drag the safe to the back of the flatbed pickup and lift it over the 3 ½ foot-high-lip. We strained every muscle we had getting that safe up and in. My part was done, so I turned to leave. Two of the guys were supposed to get into the back of Gerber's truck to cover and tie down the safe, while Gerber would be slowly driving away. Just as I got into my car, I heard all kinds of tires squealing, and then my passenger door opened and the three morons jumped in. Looking back in Gerber's direction, I realized no one had gotten in the back of the truck, another dumbass moment. I started my car and whipped around the gas station to see Gerber racing down the wrong side of the road. The safe was lying in the middle of the road back on the Landlord's street. He had taken off so fast that it slid out of the back of the truck since no one had gotten in the back to tie it down. By now I knew I needed to get the heck out of that neighborhood. I dropped the three stooges off at the nearest grocery store parking lot that I came to and headed for the next town over to clean the blood out of my car. As I was cleaning things up, I overheard some guy talking about how he had just taken his buddy into the hospital to get his arm stitched up.

So here's the outtake. The stupidity continues: bleeding arm guy went to the hospital in the same town we had just hit the house in. It was a small town, maybe 5000 people in it. It wouldn't take the hospital staff and the cops long to put that together. Next, Gerber pulled the truck into the driveway next door, instead of backing in. As he was leaving, the landlord who lived in the house was trying to pull in the driveway. Gerber spooked, had thrown the truck in forward gear and popped the clutch. So the safe went sliding out the back of the truck, right in front of a line of cars. When we came around the corner to find the safe lying in the road in front of us, there was no way we could stop to pick it up without being seen. So that's when I backed back into the gas station and went to the store parking lot and dropped the guys off. And yes the tire iron was still somewhere in the back yard.

Sensing something suspicious, the homeowner was trying to chase Gerber down all the while. Gerber finally got out of town and lost him on an old country road. Then he shoved his truck over the side of a mountain, walked home and reported his truck stolen the next morning. Of course that didn't make much sense either as the truck was over 20 years old and a piece of junk.

I left the state. I traded the car I was driving in to a junkyard I knew. After some time passed, I checked back in with someone in the town who was in the know. He told me that there was never a word said or anything in the local paper. Kind of makes me wonder what was really in "the little safe." Just goes to show you that without a solid plan, good information, and reliable people, schemes just don't turn out good.

Speaking of unreliable people, during this time period, Pam had come with me to Tennessee. But being the '70s and all, we had a very understanding "open relationship." During our time in Tennessee, she had a boyfriend named Dink she stayed with instead of me. Not much of a name compared to Rowdy, but Pam flitted to different men like a bee to the next flower. I didn't hold anything against her for what she was doing. Truth be known, I didn't feel I had any right to claim an exclusive relationship with her because I was gone so much of the time. We would get back together when she grew tired of him. So I went on my way.

Just for the record, Dink was the one with the tire iron who broke the window and cut his arm.

19

Ben's Shoot Out

I ended up in Massachusetts after the botched safe job. I went to visit Mike and Bobby to see what action they had going on. Sure enough, Bobby needed help getting a motorcycle back. I was game as soon as I heard who was going to go to do the job. It was gonna be Ben, Bobby, myself, and our driver was gonna be a State Patrolman. The State Patrolman had done a few deals with us before; mainly he had bought a little pot. He and Bobby had grown up together.

The four of us rode in the patrolman's unmarked car to the place well out in the woods where the bike was supposed to be. I'm sure the guys in the house saw our car coming down the long driveway as we approached because all the lights in the house were off when we pulled up. It was a two-story house with sliding doors going to a balcony on the second floor above the front porch.

Bobby went to the door and knocked as the rest of us hid around the front yard. When Bobby told the guy we were there for the bike, the guy told Bobby to back off or he would shoot. I couldn't really hear the conversation that Bobby and he had through the door, but I knew it was about the motorcycle and it was heated.

As Bobby and the guy continued their argument, I was looking around for some cover to stay out of any line of fire. I found a stack of firewood across the driveway in front of the house that gave me a view of the front door and the balcony. Bobby was still at the front door talking thinking the guy was on the other side of the door. The first shot came from the balcony on the second floor. The glass doors were cracked open just a little and we were being fired on from up above. Not a good position for us to be in.

Ben was still standing in the driveway and froze in that position. I guess he hoped the guy couldn't see him. As a second shot rang out, Ben spooked and started to move. The third shot found Ben. He was hit! The guy was shooting at us with a shotgun. So Ben got hit with some pellets in his left side. He went down. I jumped from behind the wood pile to grab Ben, who was a lot larger than me, and hollered for Bobby to help me get him behind some cover. As we pulled him down the driveway, I shot at the house hoping to hit the glass sliding doors. Don't know what I hit, but I didn't hear any breaking glass. Those shots did give us the time we needed though to get Ben to the car.

Our State Patrolman was already back in his car and wanting to leave. I was pissed off, some backup he'd been. He was the only other person who brought a weapon beside myself. Anyway, we got Ben in the backseat of the car. Now all of a sudden another shot rang out. The guy must have stepped out on the balcony and had a line of sight at us again. I dropped to the ground for cover. I didn't know that they were all going to leave me there by myself. With the guy shooting I wasn't about to run down the driveway and get shot in the back trying to catch the car. I figured Bobby and I would finish what we came for. The patrolman was backing the car down the driveway, and while the shooter opened up at the car, I aimed at the balcony and let loose. It was pretty dark and I really couldn't see much more than the muzzle flash with each shot, so I'm sure my aim was less than accurate. It quieted down in just a couple of minutes though. I couldn't hear any movement and could see less on the balcony.

Next was to try to find Bobby. The patrolman was long gone with Ben and I couldn't find Bobby so I assumed he had either made it to the car or was wandering around like me. After what seemed like hours, I finally gave up. With everything so quiet, I knew I needed to get out of there.

Now I was in the woods at a house that I didn't know the whereabouts of, nor where I was. I started walking through the woods very carefully. After quite time I came upon some railroad tracks. I just started following them knowing sooner or later I would find a place with a payphone. Turns out I actually came upon a cement plant.

I sat on the edge of the plant waiting for daylight. I was still hiding under plenty of forest cover so nobody could see me but I still had a good view of the whole place. Just at the break of dawn a couple of trucks came in. When the one fellow got out, I couldn't believe my luck. I knew him – he was Mike's father. I had met him in passing before but we weren't close by any means. Acting on instinct, I gave up my cover, came out of the woods, and walked right up to him. "Good morning Bud! I was hoping you would get here. The car broke down a little ways off, can I use your phone to call Mike to get some help?" I said. Bud said sure, and pointed me in the direction of the phone in his office. I could tell he was a little nervous, probably because of my appearance. I looked a little worse for wear as I had been out in the woods all night, had crawled around in the dirt back in the gunfight, and hadn't had any sleep. But I called Mike and he came and got me.

Mike had already heard about the night from Bobby. Bobby,

by the way, had gotten in the patrol car after all and rode back with everybody else. He had taken Ben to the hospital, so there was no way I could fault him for leaving anyway. Turns out since it was only a shotgun wound, Ben would be all right. But since it was a shotgun wound, I had better not go see him as the police were asking questions.

I guess it all worked out okay. No one died, but we never did get the blasted bike.

20

Police Station Pot

Since I was already in Massachusetts, I figured I would see what else was happening. Mike told me that some guys had recently gotten busted coming into West Dennis with a few bales of pot. Since we were right by the Cape, I figured, what the heck, I'll go look it over. Sometimes busted pot is the easiest to retake.

In my surveillance, I discovered that the West Dennis police station wasn't much more than an old wooden house with a garage on the side of it. I cased it during the day so I would know some of the roads in and out of the area. When it got dark, I slipped up to the garage to peak in the window. I could only see through a small scratch in the window treatment, but sure enough, two bales were stacked right there. Bobby had come along in case it was a doable job and I needed the help. As we hid in the brush watching the police station, it appeared there were only three officers on duty at night.

We decided that Bobby would be the lookout and I would go to the garage and see if I could get in the window. I had no problem getting to the window and I started to try different ways to open it without making too much noise. Then I heard a bird whistle, which was Bobby's alert that something was happening. I laid down flat on the ground to make my profile as small as possible. Then I crawled to the edge of the garage so I could look toward the door to the police station. As I looked around the corner of the building, there was a cop not 20 feet from me. I froze and tried to control my breathing. I smelt a whiff of cigarette smoke. The cop had come outside for a smoke break. Relief came over me as I realized he wasn't doing a perimeter sweep and I just needed to lie low until the he reached the end of his smoke.

Once he went back inside, I went back to the window. Not two minutes later, there came the only two patrol cars on duty screaming up to the station. Now I'm not sure if I was heard or spotted or if it even had anything to do with me. All I knew was they were coming in like gangbusters with high beams on and I wasn't sticking around any longer. I took off for the woods behind the police station.

As I was busy navigating my way away from there, I could tell they were searching for someone. Thank goodness Bobby had made his way back to the car already. I had seen him pass by on the road but he couldn't stop because the cops were between us. I was hiding in some low bushes while the cops were using their spotlight to look up through the trees and shadowy areas. After about an hour of playing the cat and mouse game, I finally jumped out after Bobby and got in the car. We cruised off the Cape over the Sagamore Bridge.

After my run of unsuccessful jobs, I needed a chance to recoup. Plus, I was ready to get back to a place where I knew things could settle down a little better. I had my sites set for Florida and a few of the guys thought they'd like to come along. It was getting to be a pretty regular trip for me, driving straight south, straight through, stopping only for gas, food, and to smoke a joint.

21

The Check Scam

When we arrived in the Sarasota area I went and rented a house on Siesta Key. By this time Pam's folks had done well with their plumbing business and bought 10 acres quite some distance out of town. They built a large new house with an indoor pool. I don't think they ever knew much about where we were. I know that Pam would call them now and again but I don't know what she told them. Pam had grown tired of Dink and came back to live with me again. Since we had moved back to Siesta Key, Pam had her friends around again. Most everyone that came by or would stay with us were people she knew. The most I would do with them is get them some pot as I didn't want them to get into trouble doing it on their own.

At that time, Store Cable TV was a big local cable company. Dale, a medium-build, redheaded hustler who I had done some prior drug deals with came to me with his latest scam. Dale had managed to get one of Store Cable TV's payroll checkbooks and check stamper. He planned to open 50 checking accounts in the closest three towns in the area. I put up some of the seed money to open the accounts and I would only be an advisor on this job. But that was mainly because

Dale wanted the majority of the deal for himself. That was all right with me because he didn't listen too well.

I advised him not to max out the amount payable on the check, which was $500. That would only draw attention to him. Besides, in those days, $500 was a pretty hefty paycheck and he had plenty of checks to go around as long as he didn't get too greedy with them.

After Dale had been around and set up most of the accounts, I introduced Dale to Brian who would be the driver. Brian was a young, skinny, blonde beach boy who always needed money. At least he had his own car.

The two of them were sitting in my kitchen stamping out the 50 checks. But Dale made all the checks out for just a few dollars short of $500. Some people just don't get it. After they were done stamping the checks, Dale put on his disguise. He had a fake beard, a hairpiece, glasses, and makeup to make him dark skinned. When he put on a baseball cap, he looked like a bank robber to me. However, I didn't say anything and away they went out to beat 50 banks.

Within two hours they were back and backing the car into my carport. After the first 10 banks or so, the drive-up tellers were on to them. At the last bank, the teller told them to wait a moment while they checked the account. In the meantime, someone walked out of the bank and tried to take down the tag number on the car. So they beat it out of there and didn't know what to do so they came to my house. Thanks a lot! Anyway I figured I had better help them get this cleaned up since the house was blown now anyway.

I got rid of the check machine and the checks. I had them park the car in the mall parking lot so it could be watched to see if the cops were looking for it. I told the guys to stay out of sight and separate as quickly as they could and to get off of Siesta Key because being on an island where there were only two roads on and off was a bad place to be in their situation, especially if they had their tag.

I never did see any money back from this mistaken deal. But then I never got any heat or trouble from it either, so I believe I did all right. Breaking even is the same as a win some days in my line of work. Everyone got away clean, which was a good thing because I'm not sure it would have turned out well if the guys had gotten caught.

22

Radio with a Cop Microphone

Since I'd use a fake name to rent the house I had no problem picking up and leaving. I packed my bag and moved off the island to the town about 20 miles away and used a different name to rent the upstairs of an old house that was on the north side of Bradenton. The house was built up off the ground with a small crawl space below it. That made it the perfect house for me at the time. You see, I was stashing product and other stuff underneath the house. That way the house inside was clean except for a little bit of pot.

I had only been there a short time and hadn't run into anyone I didn't already know. I wanted to keep a really low profile for a while, so I never let anyone come by the house or even told anyone where I was staying. I guess I must've had some heat on me that I hadn't picked up on though, because one afternoon a young man I didn't know knocked on my door. The front door was at the bottom of the stairs opening up onto a porch. When I opened the door, this younger fellow had a large boom box with him resting on the porch railing facing me. He acted as if I knew him or "the guy" who told him to come see me. He asked to buy some pot from me. I told him I had no idea what the hell he was talking about and to get the hell away from me.

He looked as nervous and novice as you could be and he turned and left. As soon as I closed the door, I knew he was either a cop or confidential informant. There was no mistaking it. I knew the moment he started to talk to me. All the questions were pre-rehearsed and meant to imply guilt.

After waiting inside the door for only a minute or two, I went back outside to look around. I needed to know how close they were and how hot I was. I didn't see anyone close around the house, so I figured they were collecting input to get me later. I jumped in my car and drove around the neighborhood.

Within a block and a half, I saw and drove right past the kid. He looked at me and turned white. I continued to the first corner and turned right. Then to the end of the block and again right. About a block and a half down there was a side street to my left. There he was, the handler, or cop rather, that had sent the kid to my door. When I stared him down, he knew his cover was blown, even if he was in an unmarked car. I drove by him real slow to make sure we made eye contact, to let him know I wanted to remember what he looked like. I drove back around to the house and went upstairs. Mine and Pam's relationship was more by way of mutual convenience at this point. Since she happened to be with me in the Bradenton house that day, I told her to pack only what she needed. At the same time, I packed my one bag and threw it in the car. I hooked the trailer up and loaded the bike and packed the car as quickly and quietly as possible. We were done and ready to go within two hours. Now I just needed to wait for darkness to get what I had stashed under the house so that we could leave without a trace.

When it was dark enough, I crawled under the house to pull

everything out. One box was missing. Well now I knew I must be really hot because of what the box had in it: notebooks with formulas and a copy of the code I would use to make certain notes to myself. It was a bad box to be missing. I grabbed the other supplies from under the house, threw them in the trunk, grabbed my girl, and took off.

I only went as far as Tampa that night where I ditched the car and the trailer. I made sure to take both tags even though I had used an alias name to buy them. I bought a pickup truck with cash and a different ID, reloaded everything and got out of the state. I didn't stop driving until Massachusetts.

23

The Stash House

The Massachusetts crew had acquired an empty house off the beaten track somewhere close to South Carver, Massachusetts. It was still like brand new. Only one family had lived in it before we got it, so it was in great condition. There was very little furniture in the house but the basement featured a great workbench.

The house was meant to be multi-purpose. It was a stash house, a hideout, a factory, and most importantly, it was supposed to appear vacant. While there were some other homes in the area, this house was situated on a large plot of land with plenty of mature trees and brush to provide cover. Just in case though, there were a long set of rules to keep the house safe. There were no vehicles to be parked in the driveway or to be seen coming or going. If you needed to access or leave the house, it would have to be done very discreetly, foot traffic only, usually through the back and on to a rendezvous down the road. All the windows in the house were blacked out so that no one could see any lights on or see inside. Also we had jumped the power to the house with jumper cables because the house had no meter. There was no way to call in or out either. For all intensive purposes, this house was off the grid.

In the basement I had a hot, and I mean a smoking hot, red motorcycle stashed. I had acquired it from a doctor with a smartass attitude. He was dealing drugs on the side and tried to rip off buyers by selling them bad product, so the buyers decided to take some of his toys to let him know he wasn't untouchable. Anyway, that's how I ended up with the bike. I didn't mind too much. It was sure a nice bike.

I was also storing some drugs in that house. In fact, I made a chair against the wall out of bales of pot. Then there were the REDS, the downers I had dealt in a lot before that were still a popular commodity. I must've had 10,000 or so in baggies of 1000 wrapped in small brown paper lunch bags.

Down in the basement where I had the motorcycle stashed, I had a full workbench and tools for making pipe bombs. I had been hired to make a couple for some people, plus I needed one for a project of my own.

One day, a couple of guys I was working with came by to ask me to go do a pickup and delivery. The job took almost all night so I didn't get back to the house until just before dawn. The guys let me off not far from the house. I had to walk the rest of the way since any traffic around the house was a big no-no. I walked along the hedge line and some overgrown grass that ran up to the back of the house. The entrance I was using was one directly into the basement, this way the front and rear doors to the house were never open. This also eliminated the possibility of tracks or paths leading to them.

After entering the basement, I relocked the basement door and went upstairs. This was when things went off track. I called out for Pam, but no answer. That made me nervous as we were the only ones in the house. My first thought was that she got mad and left, maybe just walking off down the road. Now this was a possibility because I had known her to get upset in the past and make very bad decisions. Like the time she called the FBI on me. But that's a different story. Anyway, all my concerns were nowhere close to what I was about to find.

As I walked from the kitchen into the next empty room, I saw Pam lying on the floor. At first I was relieved, thinking she was just sleeping. Boy was I wrong. As I got closer, I saw red pills spilled all over the floor so I knew it couldn't be good. At first I was pissed off that she would be so sloppy. Eat a couple of pills okay, but to dump them on the floor – NOT okay. I started to gather up the pills as I worked my way to her. She was on her side with her back to me.

When I finally reached her and rolled her over on her back, my worries were not on the pills on the floor anymore. It was apparent she had eaten way too many pills. She was nonresponsive at all. There was dried drooled down the side of her face. I put my ear to her chest and could just hear a very slow and weak heart beat. Well, that wasn't good! I knew no one was going to be back by the house for at least two days. And it wasn't like I could just walk to the neighbor and asked to use their phone. Heck! I didn't even exist as far as anyone around there knew. Here I was in a stash house with a girl who had just over-dosed, a hot motorcycle, bomb manufacturing, too much dope, and of course not to forget all the guns that I carried in those days. So what was there to do? I had to think fast for Pam's sake.

I tried all the usual stuff, put her in a cold shower, damp cloth around the neck, tried to get some water down her and anything and everything that I had ever heard or tried before. Nothing seemed to change a thing. She was still as unresponsive as ever and I was getting beyond worried. After spending a couple more hours just trying to do all the things I knew to do all over again, I decided I had to just wait it out. By now, the outcome couldn't be changed, so I went on about my work. I checked on her every couple of hours to take a damp cloth and wet her lips and to wipe her face. Other than that, I did nothing.

After analyzing the situation repeatedly while working in the basement, I figured she had tried to kill herself because she had been doing downers for as long as I had known her. She knew her limits. If she had just wanted to get high, well she sure managed that. All kinds of crazy things went through my head for the next 20 or so hours. But finally she did wake up. At that time I am not sure if I was happy, sad, or just plain mad! I was an emotional train wreck. As soon as the guys came by for their next check up, I got Pam out of that house and headed south for Florida. A life of seclusion in Massachusetts was no life for her.

Later on, Pam said she had gotten bored riding my coat tails and lying low and just took too many pills. I know she wished she had stayed in Florida. I should have never put her in that spot. Pam may have been a lot of things, but she wasn't one for the kind of underworld lifestyle I lived. From then on, it had to be her decision if she wanted to come along and she had to know the parameters of what she'd be getting herself into.

As far as everything went with the stash house: the doctor squared up with the guys who hired me to take his motorcycle. He wanted to get the bike back but I would have no part of that. I took the bike as part of the payment for my work. It ended up in another state with a new paint job, and a new set of numbers with a clean title. As for what I was making in the basement, I think all I can say is that I did what part I was paid for.

24

The Bike That Couldn't be Stolen

Instead of Florida, I stopped off in Tennessee. I was still a little shy to get back to Florida just yet so figured I would spend some time in the same town that we had tried to start that Renegade chapter in. Nobody knew that I had been thrown out of the main chapter in Florida and turned in my patch. Even though I was no longer a patch brother, that didn't mean I would not deal with them. Money is money and I was in business with them.

By this time, I had collected blank birth certificates from three states. I had the IBM typewriter ball for the years that I would make the IDs. I also had all the blank paper needed to make clean IDs to get driver's licenses in whatever state I happened to be in. I typed out a new identification and went to a small town to get a Tennessee driver's license. This town was so podunk that a Highway Patrol officer would only come by once a month and give the test and then issue you your driver's license. That was it. Easy as pie. Just like that I had another new license with another new name. It also helped that licenses were made of paper with no picture back then.

After being in a town like that for a short period of time, it didn't take long to find out who was who. This one biker fellow thought he was the baddest dude around. He let it be known that he didn't think too much of me or my biker brothers. I had been the president of the Renegade chapter there in Tennessee. He made it clear he thought I was a joke. He made the statement that no one could steal his motorcycle and if someone would try, he would shoot them.

Well if he meant that as a threat, it sure sounded like an invitation. Two weeks later Roach helped me take his bike right off the carport of his house and we stashed it. When this "bad biker dude" woke up in the morning and found his motorcycle was missing, he was madder than a wet hen. I got the word from sources around town that he was in his blue Corvette looking for me. Everyone knew where I lived. It was a trailer house sitting on a lot by itself. I made sure I was sitting on the steps outside when he drove by. He had gone around and told people he was going to shoot me. So when I saw him outside the trailer I was expecting a shoot out. I knew he was carrying a double-barreled shotgun because he showed it to someone who came by to warn me earlier that morning. I had two loaded guns on me when he drove up, so I was ready. Turns out he didn't even roll his window down. He just peeled out in the gravel and left.

So now I hooked up with Roach and borrowed Zero's wife's car. We took the backseat out and put the bike in the car. The car was a '56 Oldsmobile, so it had a spacious trunk and a big backseat. The bike, however, took up all of it. So to cover things up, we put some blankets and some old clothes and any other junk we could find that looked like it would not be out of place in the backseat of a car. Our plan was to take the bike to Virginia and sell it to some brothers that were in the club. Before we left, I had one last item of business to take care of.

There was a small four corners town just 20 minutes south of where we were and someone I knew told me that the dude we took the bike from was down there saying how he was fixing to shoot me. He was at a billiard hall/beer joint/bootlegger place. He was there getting drunk and spinning all kinds of plot, telling everybody how he'd get revenge. I loaded my sawed-off shotgun and put on my shoulder holster with my pistol and I borrowed a car. I went alone as I was not sure what would happen.

When I pulled into four corners, I was seen before I could get into the billiard hall. As I walked up to go in, some guy stepped up and locked the front door. Now this was bad. I could see through the door glass but the big picture window on the front of the joint was painted so you couldn't see in. At this point, I figured they were going to shoot at me through the glass. I took a few steps back and shot the big window. It went down in about a million pieces. I stepped right through the window and let that knucklehead know, if he ever threatened me again, I would send him to meet his maker. By that time, my adrenaline was surging. I gave a 60-second speech then turned and left.

When I got back to the trailer, Roach and I hit the highway for Virginia. As we were driving north I realized that the speedometer didn't work. As night came on I saw that the dash lights weren't working either. Not thinking too much about either problem, I continue to drive on through into the early morning hours.

All of a sudden, I had blue lights behind me. Roach caught on to what was happening and pulled the blanket up around him covering most of his face. The car's heater didn't work, so it was handy he had the blanket right there. I pulled over to the side of the road and the state trooper approached the car. The trooper asked me for my license and registration. I handed them over and he told me I was speeding and that in this county, I would have to follow him to the local town and go in front of the local magistrate. So I followed him to town.

This was around 1 am and I guess the trooper had no problem calling the magistrate on the way to town. When we arrived, the magistrate was already waiting. It was like a set up: the magistrate was in his robe and slippers and you could tell that he and the state trooper were pals. Roach waited for me in the car and I went in to find out what I was dealing with exactly.

The proceeding started with the trooper looking at the registration and saying, "I see the car is registered to your girlfriend." I guess Roach's long hair and blanket-covered body had been enough to unknowingly fool the trooper. So the trooper mistook him for the girl whose name was on the car registration. I went along with it and then agreed that I was going above the speed limit, not knowing if I really was or not since the speedometer hadn't been working. Anyway, the magistrate said the fine would be $100. Wouldn't you know I only had $60 on me and so I told him so. He suggested I go out and ask my "girlfriend" to see if she had any cash.

I went out to the car and asked Roach if he had any cash. I explained what was going on in this money hustle from the two "buddies" inside. Thank goodness he had the $40 that was needed to pay these two off.

As I walked back in and handed over the $100 to the magistrate, he smiled and said that I could go now. As I walked out, I knew that I had just been hustled. But what the heck. I had a hot bike in the car, and truth be known, Zero never told his wife he was giving us the car to take to Alexandria, Virginia. So all was good enough and we were back on the road. As the saying goes: half a pack of smokes and almost a full tank of gas!

Before we pulled out on the interstate, we stopped at a gas station and filled up. Good thing Roach had some money stashed or we'd have been toast. Once we got back on the interstate, we didn't stop until we got to Alexandria. We came in real early in the morning; there was hardly any traffic on the roads around us. We were going down the main road with lots of stoplights and most all of the lights were flashing yellow. I must have run one that wasn't because I had blue lights flashing behind me again.

I was really tired. I hadn't slept for more than a day and I had been driving the whole way. So when the police stopped us, they had us get out of the car. I believe they thought we were drinking. I told them that we had been driving all night and apologized for running the light. They commented about the car riding so low. I explained that we were moving all of our junk up here and our women would come after we found a house and we unloaded all the stuff that we brought. The two policemen looked at us and then at the car and back at us and said, we would take you in, but it's shift change and we don't want to be stuck all morning doing paperwork. So they told us go find someplace to sleep and stay out of trouble. Then they left.

At this point, we were burnt out and just wanted to find our contact, a guy called Mouse, and get this bike off of our hands. This prank was turning into a lot more headache and hassle than I had bargained for. Mouse was still a patched Renegade and he and I had become pretty good friends over the years. He was of average height but had been through a motorcycle wreck that left a big scar on his face and messed up one eye socket. His claim to fame was that he had dated a young girl named Judy who had been one of the college coeds that had been photographed in Playboy.

Anyway, we pulled into some little stop and shop convenience store. Believe it or not between Roach and I, we only had one quarter left and that was the price of a phone call. The phone number I had for Mouse was Judy's, but I was not aware of that when I made the call looking for Mouse. I dropped the quarter into the phone pay slot and dialed. A girl answered and I asked to speak to Mouse. The girl got really mad and hollered at me saying that he didn't live there anymore and slammed down the phone. I didn't even have time to tell her this was my last quarter that her number was my only contact number for Mouse. This number in fact was the only number I had for anyone in the entire area.

So now here we set. Hungry, tired, with a hot motorcycle in the back of the car at a Stop & Shop somewhere in Alexandria, Virginia and we had no idea where we were or where to go. I'd already been stopped twice by cops, and now I had no contact information. So what's a man to do? Roach stayed with the car and I went looking for some way to make a phone call. I saw a pop bottle and that started my search. After a half hour of walking up and down street alleys, looking for pop bottles, I had enough to get another quarter. That search made me nervous as hell. All the time I was worrying about the car with Tennessee tags with a hot motorcycle shoved in it and Roach a sitting duck if the cops happened to question him. We had been in the parking lot way too long.

I traded my goods in for the phone call quarter and knew I had to make that next call count so we could get out of there. We were calling way too much attention to ourselves and it was becoming obvious that something was not right. I dialed Judy's number again but this time as soon as I heard the girl answer, I quickly explained that she was my only contact and I was from out-of-state and we were broke. Thank goodness she was a good girl. She took the number to the pay phone and said she would contact someone to call me back. I found out it was Judy that I'd been talking to and she knew who I was but was still smoking mad at Mouse.

    I did get a call back on the pay phone. This contact was good, so they sent a probate to meet us and directed us to the clubhouse. It didn't take us long to sell the bike. I got a good price for it and I was more than happy to get it out of the car and out of my sight. We didn't hang around Alexandria very long because the brothers always have a way of trying to get you to spend the money that they pay you on them to party, and that wasn't going to happen with that money. We had to have something to get back home on! And besides, I didn't get along with all of them that well.

    We hit the interstate and after we were clear out a ways, we found a rest area and got some well-deserved and much needed sleep.

    We headed back to Tennessee, keeping the speed about where I hoped it needed to be. We really did need to get the car back to Zero's wife. I was sure by now that she had found out from Zero that we had used it to take a trip. It was a good trip back though. Roach and I spoke about a lot of things. In all the time I'd known him since he was 16 years old and in all the time we had spent together either hanging out or living together, we had never had any problems between us. Now there's not many a man you can honestly say that about. By now he was all grown up of course and had many stories of his own, so when we got to Tennessee he had things to do and I had things to do. I didn't ask him what he was up to, but I did tell him if he needed me, all he had to do was holler and I would always be there to help him. I was going back to Florida, so we said our goodbyes and that was that.

    Since I had gotten stopped twice on this trip, it was time to dispose of my latest Tennessee driver's license. I went back to using my William Van Sant alias, after all, that was my most secure ID. This was the one that I was married under and also had worked a job under and paid taxes under. Probably more legitimate than my real name by then. One thing about changing names is that the more I did it, the easier it became. It was purely a mental game by then. But my mind was strong enough to handle it – unless I got questioned when I was really tired. At extremely high-stress moments I would go into my slow country boy act. I would talk very slow yet direct and that would give me time to run the ID I was using through my mind. I thought of it like testing my words before saying them. I had created a mental block from ever using my real name of Larry. Even now I have to stop and force myself to be able to type it.

So at this time, to me my real name was Willim Van Sant. I mainly only used it when I knew there was very little chance of getting into trouble. I always tried to keep two identifications going: one to use that I could throw away and of course the more secure one that I would use when not working on the outside of the law.

25

A Hippy & His Pot

I had gotten word that Mike wanted to contact me about a job. As soon as I got to Florida and had a place to stay with a phone, I let my number be known so Mike could call me. Mike and I had been through a lot together, so I knew it was only a matter of time before he called me. We had mostly dealt with pot, so I figured I would try to locate some to have it on hand before he called.

I started reaching out to my usual contacts in the area. One of them said he had somebody that had a couple of bales of pot he could hook me up with. That would be somewhere between 20 to 25 pounds. Sounded good to me, just needed to check it out and see what the price was. My friend set up the meeting. When I showed up my contact wasn't there, just some high-class hippie that I had known for a few years but never really cared for. He was a smartass and he had never liked me either. Once he saw it was me that wanted to make the buy, he said he wouldn't sell it to me. That was that. Like the little sissy he was, he left.

This really pissed me off. My blood was boiling and I only had one thing on my mind: I was going to show that little punk who was in charge. I decided that if he wouldn't sell me the pot fair and square, I was just going to go take it away from him. I knew he lived over in small trailer house in the middle of a 20-acre pasture. I investigated his set up for a bit and learned that he kept his pot in a junk car parked on the property about 20 feet from his trailer.

A couple days later, once it was good and dark, I drove out to the perimeter of his pasture. I parked my car a little way down alongside the pasture and started walking towards his trailer. I took my time. I was by myself and I was comfortable. I spent the better part of a half hour quietly getting right up next to his little white junk car. Just before I approached the car, I knelt down in the tall grass and waited to see if he had a dog or some other type of alarm system. As my eyes adjusted to the dark, I started looking to see if there were any wires or bells or anything hooked to the car. As I crept to inspect the back of the car, I heard a noise coming from the trailer so I got low in the grass and froze.

All of a sudden, I saw him on top of his trailer looking all around. I knew that I was in good cover so I didn't move. It seemed like he spent half an hour on top of the trailer looking around, but I'm sure it was really only 10 minutes or so. I wondered if he had heard me and that's what brought him out to get up on top the trailer to scope things out. By getting out and going up on the trailer though, I learned that he was alone in the trailer.

His little check up had just reaffirmed in my mind that for sure, I knew I was taking the pot no matter what. I thought of how much it was gonna burn him. But there was no way that he could stop me, even if he did see me -- although I would much rather that he never knew that I was even there. After he was back inside the trailer for 10 or 15 minutes. I crept up to the back of the car and checked the trunk. Of course it was locked. I had my key set with me so got to work picking the lock. I popped it right open on the first little jiggle and twist. Now I was just hoping that it wouldn't make too much noise as I started to lift the trunk lid. I opened that lid so slowly that it didn't make a sound.

Inside the trunk were two full bales of pot just sitting there. I slowly picked them up and set them on the ground. I ever so slowly lowered the lid down on the trunk. The noise that the trunk made when it clicked shut may as well have been a gun shot it was so loud to me. I guess that was just because I was on such high alert though because it wasn't loud enough to notify him. Nonetheless, I scooped up the two bales, one under each arm, and sauntered away.

The next day, I heard through the grapevine about how somebody had robbed him. The story told was much more colorful than what really happened. I never said a word to anyone and I didn't sell the bales local.

26

The 36' Wooden Chris Craft

I finally got that call from Mike. But instead of pot, he needed a guard. Good to know I had gotten two free bales of pot out of trying to be prepared though. Since he didn't need any pot, I sold the two bales to a guy named Richard who was on his way to Tennessee. Then I went to meet Mike in Southeast Florida.

At the meeting, Mike introduced me to a boat captain named Dave and we looked over the boat we would be using for this job. The boat was a 36-foot, wooden Chris Craft with a forward cabin. It was an older boat but it had been washed and cleaned so it looked to be in good shape. It had two huge Lehman Ford engines, which use a lot of fuel. We went over all the regular questions: Had the boat been out on a shakedown run? What was the fuel tank size? What safety equipment and navigation did it have? We looked at the included charts and of course the compass. But none of that was supposed to be my job. Captain Dave was in charge of all the mechanical and fuel capacity, consumption, and all. I was just the muscle.

The job was to take the boat to Bimini to meet the "old man." That was the only name we had for our connection in Bimini. We would spend the night there and load the pot during a fishing trip the next day and then make a slow return trip back to South Florida.

We started south down the intercostal to get as far south as necessary for a short trip across the Gulfstream. We were coming out of Jupiter headed south. When we got to our jump-off place to start East toward Bimini, the captain didn't want to stop for fuel reasoning it was only 50 miles and we should've had plenty of fuel. At that very moment I got a real bad feeling about Dave. I had the feeling he was scared, paranoid, or stupid but not sure of which. Anytime I did a job, I always wanted to error on the side of caution and make sure I had thought of everything and prepared for every possible hang up.

Not being a fool, I had already charted our course to Bimini for my own personal reference so I knew what our heading should be. Not being an experienced seaman, I had no idea what our speed would be. As we slowly made our way down the intercostal, we smoked some pot and drank a couple of beers, but not enough to really affect anyone considering it took us over six hours to move down the intercostal. We were going at a sea slug's pace. I was under the impression that we would be there in less than four hours. Besides, I had hoped not to start across at night.

Finally, night descended and we made it out of the intercostal heading East out of the inlet going against 2- to 3-foot chop that looked more like 3- to 5-foot chop to me. Oh well, large boat and two engines, no problem. We ran the heading all night long. The best I could figure we had to be running between 4 to 6 knots. Just before daylight, we spotted a flashing light on the horizon. By this time, I was fairly unhappy with how the job was going. I told Dave if he didn't know where we were then he needed to head for the light. We should have easily found Bimini already.

Three hours later and we still weren't quite to the light and yes we had just run out of fuel. The wind had died down so I dropped anchor and the boat came to a stop. We were near a north light beacon, north of where we should have been. There we were: a boat out of fuel, unwilling to alert customs via the coastguard, and not really sure what to do to get help. So now it was time for me to stop being polite to this Captain Dave and do what I could do.

Since I had been in this area a few times before (running loads of pot through), I remembered that they had a lot of fishing tournaments going on in this area of Bimini. I knew some guys who worked the fishing tournaments on a regular basis, so I took a chance and got on the radio and made an open call to the fishermen in the area. I got lucky right away. The first callback was from a boat called the Flying Tiger. I had met them before; they were a good solid crew. They were straight, or almost straight, but they knew who I was and that's what was important at this time. They were tournament fishing and after they were finished for the day they would come tow us in. So we sat dead in the water until after 4 o'clock in the afternoon. But at least we had a plan.

When the Flying Tiger got to us, I was more than ready to get going. I took our 500-foot towrope out of the bin (that had been supposedly pre-checked by Captain Dave), and it didn't take long to see it was dry rotted. It broke pretty quick, but luckily the Flying Tiger had enough tow rope for us to use. So we tied it onto the bow of our boat and tossed it to the first mate on the Flying Tiger. I pulled anchor as quickly as possible and off we went. By now it was obvious that "Captain" Dave was a know-nothing dumbass. I was ready to kick Mike's ass for lying to me about the boat being "turn-key ready," and that the captain knew what he was doing. It was clear by then that none of that was true.

We finally reached Bimini after about an hour. I checked in with the dock master with a fake identification. I paid him well to limit our interaction with him and ensure that everything else would go smooth. It was about time to get off that boat. We headed to the bar where we were supposed to meet the "Old Man." Since our timetable had been thrown off, all we could do was make it known to the bar locals that we were around and then I went back to the boat.

A 40-foot Morgan Sailboat was docked behind our vessel. As I walked by it, I saw an old buddy of mine, Tim. He had been my first mate on a few smuggling runs. Wait until he heard this joke! We talked for a while and I told him about coming in north of the island, which was bad news out in the middle of the ocean. So he suggested he take a look at our compass. It was off almost 16°.

By evening when our contact still hadn't shown, I was getting a little nervous. We stood out like a sore thumb. Everyone around knew we were waiting on a load. Finally, I called Mike from Bimini (which by the way is not what you want to do when you plan on bringing a load back to the states.) When I talked to Mike, he said the deal had fallen through and that we should come on back.

I was furious! No deal equals no payday. What else could go wrong? What was going on here? It wasn't like Mike to set me up in such a bad scenario, and then have no payout on top of it all. Dave was angry also but he had too much rum in him to care for now.

We went to the bar, got good and drunk that night, and left around mid-afternoon the next day. The weather report said all clear till late night or early the next morning. With good weather we figured we should reach Florida in about eight hours. Besides, after fueling the tanks we had hardly any money left so we had to get going in hopes of hitting the states under the cover of darkness so no one would see us coming and start asking questions. Even though we weren't loaded, we didn't want to draw any attention.

After we got away from Bimini and out into the Gulfstream, it was rougher than we expected. We were fighting wind and waves and only making about 4 knots. At this rate it would take 10 to 12 hours to get to West Palm Beach. About halfway across, we started hitting 4- to 6-foot waves and in total darkness of course. A couple of hours later, the waves were coming over the bow of the boat. Our bad situation just kept going from worse to critical. The front hatch on the bow gave way next as a large wave pounded us and snapped it completely off. Now we had real problems! Every wave over the bow put gallons of water in the forward cabin. I went down below into the forward cabin to see what I could find to cover the open hatch. I scrounged up a hammer and a few nails but no wood, so I ripped a cabinet door off of the sink cupboard. We were now rolling and pitching so hard it took me forever to pre-start the nails in an effort to speed things up once I got topside.

It didn't matter though cause there was no way I could stay atop the bow in that weather. I would have been washed overboard without a prayer. Next best option was to nail it from inside and below deck. As I worked my way forward, I realized I was a foot deep in water. Below the hatch was nuts. When the bow of the boat dipped forward, the water was almost 3 feet deep and pouring in the hatch at the same time. By the time I got the board nailed to the bottom of the hatch, all kinds of stuff was floating in the cabin with me. I shoved a pole between the floor of the cabin and a hardback cushion against the cabinet door I had nailed to the bottom of the hatch. Some water was still getting in, but not much.

When I went through the main cabin getting back topside, the water was almost up to my knees. I came out on deck to find Dave puking his guts out and looking really bad. At the moment there was nothing I could do for him. I was getting a 5-gallon bucket and opening the engine compartment from the deck so I could bail water from the engine room. Everything was up to me.

As I was down in the engine room bailing water, I heard a thud from up above. It was Dave falling over onto the deck. I ran up on deck and grabbed the wheel to point the bow of the boat back into the waves so we wouldn't run parallel to them and flip. With just one of me, all I could do was keep the wheel steady while watching Dave slide all over the deck passed out. I took a rope and tied the wheel to keep the bow pointed sort of the right direction, then shimmied over to the stern and grabbed Dave who was out cold. I took the other end of the rope and tied Dave to the deck cleat so he wouldn't get thrown overboard. Then it was back to bailing water. As I checked the wheel one last time before going below, I saw that the switch on the bilge pump was off. How long it had been off I didn't know but at least I was able to flip it on!

Back down in the engine room I was in way too much water. I was bailing for my life, when one of the engines died. There was nothing I could do but keep bailing water. I don't know how long I bailed water, but somewhere along the line, the other engine died too. It didn't matter now; I just had to keep bailing.

By the time I got the water down below the engine mounts, I realized the bow wasn't pitching anymore. We were riding smooth swells. It was late into the night, maybe even early morning, I wasn't sure. All I knew was that I needed to get at least one of those engines started. I opened the distributor cap and after some time got it dried out. Since everything in the boat was soaked, the only thing I could find dry was the toilet paper we kept in a plastic bag. Lesson well learned: always have dry paper! After a while, I did get the one engine started. Hallelujah!

I had no idea how far north we had drifted. I just looked to the west, picked out a star and used it for my heading. As the sun started to come up behind me, I could see that I was coming in very close to the inlet I wanted to by West Palm Beach.

I limped the boat back to the dock behind Mike's house. The boat was a wreck. I really didn't care; I was alive and back on solid ground. Dave was still out or dead and I really didn't care about that either. I just left him tied to the deck; he didn't deserve any better. He was a big part of the problem we had been in such dire circumstances, and then he had gone and left me to deal with everything.

I went right into Mike's house. It was early morning and I walked right into his bedroom to find him sleeping instead of up keeping watch for us. I was pissed! I told him his boat was at the dock and I was leaving. I stormed out of there before I killed Mike for his carelessness.

Later, Mike had the gall to call me hollering about how I had destroyed his boat. I couldn't believe I had to listen to his bull crap, so I told him he was lucky I hadn't slit his throat when I found him asleep when he should've been awake and on point. He was lucky I was already on the West Coast and in a cooling down period by the time he phoned or else I may have gone back there and done just that. It was again time to regroup and throw away the ID papers that I had used in Bimini on the dock master. Once again I would be William Van Sant.

27

Ambush at The Red Barn

Since I was on the West Coast of Florida I decided to go visit Roach who had moved back to the area. I was with him when he got his first patch. That was the start of his love for motorcycles and brotherhood. After the ordeal I had just been through, I needed to be among friends – real friends – and Roach was as good as family for me.

I visited him at the Outlaw clubhouse that Roach was a part of. We had a lot to catch up on since we were last together and it wasn't long before we ran out of beer. I'm not quite sure how we decided that I would leave my guns behind for the beer run, except I was elected to go and buy the beer so maybe it was better to not be packing and paying. Since there were only six of us at the clubhouse, five guys and Pam, we all jumped into the van and took off.

I'm not quite sure where or when the Renegades spotted us. The Outlaws' clubhouse was in Bradenton, Florida and the Outlaws were trying to move in and claim Bradenton for their own. It was a flat out turf war. I was always welcome wherever Roach was, and the Outlaws had always treated me well so I thought nothing of hanging out anywhere with Roach or the Outlaws. Since I wore no patch I was no threat to any of them.

After going to a place called The Red Barn, two of us went in and bought the beer. We returned to the van and were leaving as a car pulled up beside us and told our driver, Roach, to F-off. Roach knew the guy and knew he was from his rival club. The car turned right on the main highway and sped off down the road. Roach took a right and was after him. There were three people in the car. I guess Roach thought the odds were in our favor.

As we were chasing after them, they made a right turn into a housing project. At that moment my radar went off. I was in the back of the van and I hollered up to Roach to stop following them because it was an ambush. Everyone in the van except Pam had some smart remark to throw back at me. We were making too many rights and lefts to be in control anymore. We were winding ourselves in too deep in the neighborhood to make an easy get away. I told Pam to lie down on the floor of the van and I put an old blanket over her. Next I rolled the spare tire over and positioned it resting on the wheel well covering as much of her as possible. I was pissed that Pam had been drug along and was in the middle of all this.

I asked Wolf, who was riding shotgun, for his pistol since I was the better shot. He refused and I grabbed for it anyway which got us both arguing real good. Just then, the car in front of us sped up like they were trying to lose us. Instead, the driver swung the car sideways in front of us in the street. There was no way to get around them. Just as we passed an alleyway, a van pulled out sideways blocking our rear exit. I was looking out the back window trying to see what was coming. I started hollering for everyone to get down. No one listened. Roach's younger brother was looking out the back window. As I took a last look, the doors slid open on the van behind us and two gunmen with rifles jumped out. My face hit the floor of the van and bullets started flying.

Shots rang out for only a few moments, yet that was plenty long enough. The car and other van peeled off. We checked everyone before we left too. Roach's little brother got hit in the side of his back and was down but still alive. We took him to the hospital as fast as we could. Roach and I carried him through the emergency room doors, took him straight into a bed in the hallway, and hollered out that he had been shot. Then we got the hell out of there. Roach's brother lived through this ordeal even though he had been shot in the lung, only to die a couple of years later jumping off a boat while partying with some brothers. After a while you get used to seeing or hearing about death all around you. Hell, with the number of times I should have died myself, death, dying, and killing weren't any shock. Your skin just thickens up tougher than your chaps after a while because it no longer seems to bother you.

After we left the hospital, we went back to the Outlaw clubhouse to clean up some items and then get clear out of there. While there, Wolf and myself had a very heated argument over his actions during the shooting. It turned out that I would discover years later that Wolf was actually planted by the Feds to infiltrate the Outlaw motorcycle club. That's why he wouldn't give me his pistol, and that's why he never returned fire when the Renegades ambushed us. At least I was glad he got the crap scared out of him.

The day after the shooting we watched the news to see how it would get reported. The shooting was supposedly done by "unknowns." One of the bullets had passed through the front door of a couple's house and lodged in the wall in their living room. I'm sure the cops knew the shooting was between two bike clubs, so not much of an investigation seemed to follow. I suppose the cops were hoping we would make their job easier and all kill each other. So much for a trip to The Red Barn to buy a case of beer.

28

A Shot Fired in Daytona

It was early spring 1978 and that meant Daytona Bike Week was coming fast. That was the next trip on my agenda. Everybody that was anybody in the biker world would be there. I had quite the crew coming for the big week. Bobby and Mike, plus half a dozen of their guys, were coming down from New England. We went way back to their first Florida trip with those motorcycles I scrounged up for them.

Pam and I, plus a few others, had rooms in a cheap hotel southwest of Daytona. It was great at the end of a ride or a long day to have a hot shower and a bed. That was the only good thing you could say about the dive hotel we were in. I'm not sure who was in charge of our room more: the cockroaches or us. Since it was Daytona bike week, every fleabag hotel within 100 miles had rooms for rent and this one must've been among the worst.

Of course, this was 1978. It was the decade of sex, drugs, and rock 'n roll. There were plenty of drugs floating around, and it seemed that sex, but not always with your regular partner, followed that, all set to the background music of acid rock. One night, that is exactly how our evening was starting.

I had been in downtown Daytona most of the day on my motorcycle. I was riding an old Harley with a jockey shift so it was best ridden alone. That seemed to be all right as Pam and Bimini Mike were busy getting high and not caring about much else. Mike and I had made our peace once we'd both had some space. Some people you work with in my line you just have to make peace with so they don't get any ideas to screw you over as a way of exacting revenge for whatever perceived injustice occurred. Even if he was an idiot. I had to know when to let things go, when to get some space, and when to exact retribution. Mike was lucky he fell into the forgiveness category.

He had a high top van that you could stand up and walk around in. It was also equipped with a bed in the back. We had used his van on many trips since it was good for sleeping after your turn driving. That way, we never had to stop. But that wasn't what it was being used for that night.

Mike and Pam and a few other people who had come back to the motel parking lot were partying in the van. I rode in and parked by the room I was staying in. I saw Mike's van in the parking lot and thought nothing of it as I had a good pot buzz going myself. I opened the hotel room and no one was inside. So I walked over to the van and opened the side door to see what everybody was up to. I found out all right. I had just interrupted a raucous orgy set to screaming guitar music and heavy drum beats. Everybody stared at the open door and started freaking out, so I quickly closed the door.

I turned around and went back to the motel room and started to unload my gear. I guess I had missed the invite. I took off my vest and hung it on a chair by the dresser. Then I took off my shoulder holster and put it and my .38 charter arms revolver on the dresser in front of the mirror. As I was pulling my boots off, in walked Pam.

She started right in on me. "Where have you been all day!?" She screamed. "I have been stuck here with nothing to do all day." Now her complaints fell on deaf ears. I had seen some of the guys downtown and they told me Pam had been riding around with Mike and some others that day. Besides that, I had just seen Pam in the van having a lot to do. So I just blew her off and finished getting undressed to get in the shower. The whole time Pam would not stop screaming about how everything was my fault. I got in the shower and heard the door slam shut and figured she would go back to partying with Mike and crew. Just a few minutes later I heard a gunshot! It sounded like it was right outside my bathroom window.

I grabbed a towel and did a half way dry off so I could pull on my pants. I noticed my pistol wasn't on the dressed by the mirror where I had left it. I ran out the door and around behind the motel as fast as I could. Right there, just outside the bathroom window, was Pam sitting on the ground leaning against a tree. The damn fool had shot herself in the gut. She said she had tried to shoot herself in the heart, but the pistol trigger was too tough so she missed her mark. Next thing she said to me was, "This serves you right." At that moment I thought that was a strange thing for her to say. I chalked it up to emotional, high, unstable females.

An ambulance pulled up moments later and there were all kinds of people standing around. By the time they got her loaded and told me what hospital they were going to, cops were on site. With all the out-of-towners around, I think the police had been overloaded all week. Maybe they were trying to figure out what was going on, but they weren't having a lot of luck getting to the bottom of things or figuring out who was who. I went back to my room without even being stopped, got my clothes on, and went to the hospital before anyone asked me anything.

Turns out that the cops thought I shot her, but they weren't sure since they were just piecing bits and pieces of the scene together. Pam went right into surgery so the cops didn't get to ask her anything. I was in the waiting room for a while before I realized the other guy in the room with me was a plain-clothes cop. I thought it was unusual that there wasn't anyone else in the waiting room. After all, it was Daytona bike week. There had to be other people getting hurt with all the bikes in town. Broken legs, head trauma, ODs, something. It came clear to me when I went down the hall to use the bathroom. As I walked down the hall another guy stepped out of a room and started following me. That's when things clicked and I knew they were tagging me. I passed a makeshift waiting room with all types of people and kids in it staring at me as I walked by. There was a sign on the door scrawled on a piece of 8.5 x 11 paper that said "temporary waiting room." So I just took it easy and waited out the next four hours. I guess it was nicer to wait in peace and quiet anyway.

After Pam got out of surgery and could talk to the cops, she cleared it all up and told them that she had shot herself. At first they didn't believe her because she had no powder burns on her hands when she first came in. With a gunshot they always checked the person shot for powder burns. The cops thought she was afraid to say that I had done it. But after a while, they must've believed her because a cop walked in and spoke to my buddy in the waiting room and then the two of them left.

The aftermath of Pam's drama, besides implicating me, was she'd have to wear a colostomy bag for the next year while her insides healed up. Then they'd have to go back in and reconnect her intestines. I learned a good lesson though: when I take a shower with an angry woman around, my pistol will be in the bathroom with me and I will lock the door. So much for carefree fun in the sun at Daytona.

After I got Pam back to Florida's West Coast and had her all settled in, I got a call from Bobby up in Massachusetts. Time to see what he was up to.

29

Collecting $50,000 The Hard Way

Bobby wanted me to come up to Massachusetts and help him with a problem he was having. I arrived about 30 hours later. After a couple of hours of sleep to clear my head, I got the rundown on what the problem was. They had loaned this guy in Boston $50,000 to go to Hawaii and bring back a load of pot. They knew he had returned but was avoiding them. They wanted me to help them correct this problem. I was in and started to lay out my plan.

I decided I would go to collect the money. Since he didn't know me, it would make it harder for him to avoid me. If he didn't pay when I showed up, I would have to take him with me. That meant I needed a place that was secure and out of the way. There was a basement in an old hotel in Onset that was empty that would be perfect. So I prepared everything up there: food, water, and a silent room.

We went into Boston just as it was getting dark. We drove by the townhouse apartment where our mark lived. After circling the neighborhood, we stopped and knocked on the door. When he opened the door, three of us went in: the two moneylenders and myself.

Turns out the guy had a wife and two kids. One of the lenders took them into a room to keep them out of the conversation while we discussed the situation with Mr. IOU. None of us had brought any weapons, so we put Mr. IOU in a bedroom for the questioning. While I asked him about the money, the product, their whereabouts, and the trip, the other lender searched the house to see if he could turn anything up. As I was trying to put the fear of God into this man, I came to the conclusion that the money or the product was not in the house. He was too sure of himself and he wasn't cracking. We would not get what we came for.

It was time to go. As I tied his hands and put a pillowcase over his head, I could see the fear set in on his face. It took us an hour to get to the place in Onset.

There was a low entrance to the place we were going to keep him. The basement of the hotel was divided into dark, dirty little rooms without windows and a single light bulb with a pull cord for a switch. The place was supposed to be scary and intimidating and I thought Mr. IOU was gonna pee his pants. After I got him inside, I handcuffed him to a nasty old solid wooden couch, and then took the pillowcase off his head. Now he was alone with me and had no idea where he was. I could tell by his nervous flinches and jerky movements that he was getting pretty worried.

I made up my questioning strategy as I went along. I hoped he would just pay back the money or cough up the pot. Since he wasn't cooperating, I could see I needed to shake him up a little bit to get some answers. I was to be the only one he saw for at least 20 hours a day and I would not let him sleep during that time. Then one of the other two would come and play the good guy. They would tell him that I was crazy and the only way to get out of this place was to pay back the money. Then they would offer to let him make a phone call, give him a little water, and something to eat. They would make sure he stayed awake too.

Meanwhile, during my short break, I was sleeping in another room in the hotel. When I came back after the first day of this, I let him know I was real angry that I had to come back. Halfway through the second day, he was ready to make the call for the money. Since there were no cell phones in those days, I had to mess with him until one of the guys showed up with the phone set up. I had been poking him with a broom handle to keep him awake. He was more than happy to see my replacement show up.

We had placed a phone in the next room with a 25-foot cord so we could let him make the call. The hotel was hardwired for phones in every room, it was just that we didn't want him to have any idea he was in an old hotel. He thought he was in an underground bunker of some type. So I left one of the guys with him so I could grab some sleep while he made his first phone call. By now, after not letting him sleep for almost 2 days, he was getting a little goofy. But it seemed to work. Whomever he spoke with was ready to set up the payment.

I came back after my four hours of sleep and made sure I kept him awake. In just a couple of hours, the guys came back and said the money had been paid. So the pillowcase went back over Mr. IOU's head and we returned him to Boston. They dumped him out it a district called the combat zone. It was a late night party place with all bars and lots and lots of hookers. It was called the combat zone because of all the crime and bad guys that hung out down there. I know that being there must have scared this high-class Bostonian half to death, especially after what he had just been through and going off of no sleep for the last few days.

With the job done, everyone got what they were after. I got paid well, so I was headed back south after eight hours of good sleep. I decided to travel back through Tennessee.

30

The Feds were Watching

I headed for Tennessee again to meet up with Gerber. I had heard that he had a large amount of Quaaludes he wanted to move. Since it wasn't a "little safe" he was wanting to move, I figured I would be up for a piece of that action.

When I arrived in Sparta, I parked my car in a barn out in the country. I would usually pay the owners with product to be allowed to park in their barn, but this time all I had was cash. It was safer to park the car than to drive it around with Florida plates on it. I didn't want to draw any attention to myself while I was in town.

I got a hold of Gerber and we started to work out the deal. "Doing a deal" was never as simple as it sounds. You can't just "do it." It takes a lot of planning, especially if you wanted it to be successful. Turns out the guys who had the product were from Atlanta. They were a crew who just hit drug stores pharmacies. They would take what they wanted to use and sell the rest.

Gerber was the middleman on this and I was the moneyman on this particular deal. Once we had sorted out all the facts behind the real deal, we bartered back and forth through Gerber until we came to an agreement on price. Gerber was in the middle to protect them from me and me from them. That way, Gerber made his cut and the rest of us never saw each other.

I wanted to buy 10,000 Quaaludes. Once the price was agreed on, we set the location for the deal to go down. I gave Gerber the cash to go make the buy and in the meantime I set up a buyer to purchase them from me. Once Gerber came back with the Quaaludes, I got in his white van with him and we headed for Cookeville. I had set up a buyer to meet us at a diner near the highway. That way we could do our deal and he could be on his way. Sounds easy, right? Wrong!

As we drove along the country road in the Tennessee hills, I heard and saw a small fixed-wing airplane. At first I didn't think much about it. But about a half hour later, it was still close enough that you could hear the engine. Now I knew something was wrong. The damn plane was watching us. I didn't know if the heat was coming from the Atlanta crew or somewhere else. Turns out the Feds were watching both us and the Atlanta boys and trying to get our entire circle of people spotted and set up to take down.

I told Gerber we were being followed and he thought I was crazy. When we got to Cookeville I had him pull into a motel like we were going to stay. The motel was built on a bluff above the road with only one entrance and the bluff hid the parking lot from the road. After we'd parked, I walked to the north side of the lot to look over the bluff down onto the entry road. There sat a dark tan car with one man inside. You could tell by looking it over that it was an unmarked police car. I looked at the man inside the car who took one look at me and whipped a U-turn and sped away. I figured now that they knew we were on to them it was a good time to make a move while they regrouped.

We left the motel parking lot double quick and headed back

to where my car was stashed in the barn. Gerber and I said "see you later" and he was off with no more than a slow down for me to get out with my bag of pills. Gerber and I agreed that he would head northeast for an hour or so to hopefully draw the heat away from me. Since Gerber had no product in the van with him, he should have no problem even if they stopped him. I gave him $500 for his part in the deal.

I felt pretty safe as Gerber had never seen the car I was driving to know what color or make it was. Funny thing is, it looked like the one the fed was in only a lighter shade of tan. I never did meet the buyer that was going to meet me in Cookeville. He was long gone. We did speak later and he was glad I didn't bring any problems his way. So I got on the road and headed south back to Florida. I had no problem selling the Quaaludes there.

31

The Corvette

After being back in Florida a while, I got a call from a man named Scott who wanted to know if I would sell a hot Corvette. Scott was a cousin to Dale who had been one of the two gentlemen involved in the check scam that didn't work out so well. He was a dark-haired, wiry little guy who reminded me of a weasel. Nonetheless, we had come to an agreement on the money split that we would do with the Corvette.

He had a lawyer lined up that wanted to pull an insurance job on his Corvette. Insurance jobs were the happening thing in the late '70s. If you had a payment that you wanted to avoid, you just made your car disappear. In return, you'd get a fat payout from the insurance company. It was like free money. This lawyer was going to drive his Corvette to Key West and go on a cruise. He gave Scott a key prior to going on his three-day boat ride, then headed out without another thought about it.. Scott took a bus to the Keys and an hour after the lawyer sailed away, Scott started driving back up in the Corvette to meet up with me just south of Tampa. After meeting up, we headed for Alabama to a small town where I had set up a car dealership under yet another alias a couple of years prior when I had needed to wash some money. It was a good business move for me and was sure coming in handy once again in this venture. I had picked up a VIN number of the same year Corvette so we'd be ready to title and tag it when we got to my dealership in Alabama.

I was running blocker for Scott in a red '69 El Camino with a black vinyl top. It was a four-speed with a 396 motor so it was fast enough that if the cops started to tail Scott, I would create a diversion by speeding off and distracting the cops away from him. Also for this ride I made sure to keep my "legit" alias, William Van Sant, clear so I was using a burner ID with an Indiana birth certificate to ensure I didn't have any Florida or Alabama ties.

Both Scott and I had brought our girls along with us since we thought this would be a pretty easy run. I had Pam riding with me and Scott had his girlfriend riding with him. Just as we were getting out of the Florida panhandle, some motorcycles came along beside us, passed by, then slowed down to come alongside me. Low and behold it was Rock, the national Northeast secretary and treasurer for the Banditos. I used to be his Sgt. at arms (bodyguard) back when I wore their colors. He was still a Bandito though and I had retired long ago. I rolled down the window and we hollered our hello's back-and-forth then he invited me to their clubhouse. I didn't want to draw any attention to our situation or have to involve anybody else, so I told him to lead the way.

It was good talking about old times with him back at the clubhouse. While we were all hanging out, I slipped out to the backyard and drilled out the number plate on the Corvette and put the new VIN numbers in place. That made me feel pretty secure since it would be hard for any cops to make a solid connection without a matching VIN. I partied the night away with peace of mind.

From there, we went to the courthouse in the small Alabama town where the car dealership was set up. Doing a title transfer went off without a hitch. So now that we had a legal registration and legal tags it was time to sell the Corvette. Over to Tennessee to find a buyer. I had a Chevy dealership in mind I was sure would buy the car. I didn't bother contacting him because I had done business with him before and knew he would take it.

We arrived in the Chevy dealer's town in Tennessee and checked into a motel on the edge of town. Scott and the girls got settled into the motel while I went to set up the contact and do some other business I had prearranged that didn't affect the others.

While I was gone, Scott and the girls got drunk, high, and a little loose. There was a bit too much naked play, and way too much intoxication because Scott's girlfriend told him she wanted to be with me at some point. He got mad, took off speeding and spinning out and ended up getting his car, the Corvette, high-centered on some rocks. A highway patrolman threw him in jail and towed the car to the Chevy dealership – the same one I was going to sell the car to.

The next morning, shortly after 8 am, a guy who knew me tracked me down and said he had just been released from jail at 7 am. He warned me that he had been locked up with some guy saying all kinds of things about me and that I had better get gone before anything went down. So that's how I found out about the wreck. I went and moved the girls to the basement apartment where I had spent the night before.

Then I was off to the Chevy dealership. I met the owner as he opened at 10 am. I needed to search the car before the Highway Patrol came to look at the car. There was a .38 pistol hidden in the car that I didn't want them to find. After that was cleaned up, I turned to the dealership owner and made the only deal left. It went from a $10,000 deal to a $1500 deal. A hot, wrecked Corvette is not worth much. He had all the bargaining chips on his side, so I had to know when to cut my losses to save face.

With that taken care of, I went back to the basement to sort things out with the girls and get gone. I gave Scott's girl $800 and told her to go bail him out of jail. She said, "Screw that! I love you and want to go with you!" After some talking, I convinced her she needed to be the one to go bail Scott out and I'm sure we'd see them again at some point back in Florida. Crying, she finally agreed and damn was I glad. Enough with the female problems.

So I got into the El Camino with Pam and headed south back to Florida. I needed to get out of sight and out of mind of the Sparta police. There was a history there already and I didn't want to add to it.

You might think the story of Scott and the Corvette is over. I did too, but not so lucky. The second part starts in Florida two years later.

Dale, Scott's brother, happened to see me one afternoon and asked how he could get a hold of me later. I gave him a phone number that he could leave me a message on. You see at that time, I never had a phone in my name and I mainly used payphones. However, there were a couple of people I would regularly talk to to see if I had any messages left for me. The main contact number I used was Jackie's. She had straightened out pretty good and married a contractor named Danny. They had a stable house, were straight, and so it was always a good contact number.

A few days later, Dale called me and said he had a deal for me. He had $25,000 worth of pot and asked if I could move it. I said all right, let me get a look at it. We agreed to meet in the early afternoon the next day on a gravel road southwest of town where some old farmhouses were.

As I was going down the gravel road to the meet up, I saw Dale standing by his car with the hood up. I pulled around in front of the car on my '76 shovel head with a kick start and Jockey shift and parked my bike at a 45° angle for easy departure. As I dismounted my bike, Dale had a plastic jug in his hand and said his car had overheated. He pushed the jug my way pointing off the road and asked me to go down to the creek that was down there to get some water. It seemed a little strange, especially since as he was talking, I had walked to the front of the car and looked over the radiator. It was full of water and the engine wasn't hot.

I knew something was wrong. I turned to hop back onto my bike, taking a quick look at Dale as I did so. He looked a little pale and sweaty. I stepped on my bike, started it up and turned back the way I had come from on the gravel road.

As I started to ride off, Scott came out of the woods pointing a .38 pistol at me and hollering something at me about how I had screwed him over on the Corvette deal. He blocked my path, grabbed the bike key, turned it off, turned around and threw it into the woods where he had been hiding earlier. As he turned away to throw the keys in the woods, I dug into my pocket and took out my second key. I turned the ignition on and started the bike on the first kick. I hit the clutch and kicked it into gear just as Scott's first shot went off. He had turned back toward me as the bike started. I believe he was afraid to shoot me, so he was shooting at the bike and hit my rear tire. I took off anyway. Flat tire on a gravel road, no problem if I could get some speed up. As I tore away, the second shot went off and then a third. By this time, the bike was screaming. Two more shots had gone off and none had hit me. That was five. He was empty and I was gone.

Later I found a bullet had gone through the top of my oil bag less than an inch below my thigh. One of the other shots hit the bike frame and stuck there.

Anyway, I was nearing the end of the gravel road and unsure if Scott and Dale were following me. I made a left turn onto the paved road, but that gave me a real problem. Flat tires don't do so well on asphalt, especially after such a hard left turn. Half a mile down the road I knew I had to get off. Making another hard left into a driveway, I put the bike in a carport between a parked car and the door of the carport to the house. I knocked on the door as I shut the bike off, hoping that this stranger would harbor me for a while.

An elderly lady opened the door and I stepped right past her inside. I could see she was a bit nervous so I spoke very calmly, "I have a flat could I please use your phone and I'll be right out of here?" I saw the phone on the table by the couch so I didn't wait for an answer. I stepped to the phone and made the call as she anxiously watched me.

When my buddy Don answered the phone, (he was one of my brothers from back when I was a Renegade that I now made deals on the side with) I said, "I have just been ambushed and my tire is flat! They shot the damn thing out. Bring the van and the guns." I turned to the elderly woman and asked the house address. She gave it to me and I gave it to Don and the call was over.

The guys were there in 15 minutes. We loaded the bike and I thanked the woman.

We did a quick sweep of a 5-mile radius to make sure everything was clear. We watched the old lady's house off and on for a half hour to make sure I wasn't spotted there. I didn't want anything or anyone to bother her after she had helped me.

After making sure everything was all clear, we went to Jackie's house, which was the phone number I had given Dale. Knowing that was the only phone number he had for me; I was hoping that he would call. It didn't take long. Sure enough, Dale called. When I took the receiver, I yelled, "What the hell was that?" The phone went silent on the other end so I told Dale we'd have a proper meeting and get this all straightened out for good. Dale said he would talk to Scott and let me know. Then the phone went dead.

When he called back, he said to me that the two of them had to leave right away to take care some business and they didn't have time to meet me. I suppose that was the safest for them since I was really pissed still.

The next day I went to see Ted, his wife, and their kids. Ted was Scott and Dale's cousin. Before Ted and his wife had kids, we used to deal some pot. We were both working our straight jobs, me as a plumber, and he as a delivery driver, and we were careful to not let on about our drug dealing. After a while, we got closer, and had a good laugh about how we were both in the same industry underneath. That's when we started dealing more and Ted introduced me to Scott and Dale. But now that Ted and his wife had kids, he straightened out, went to work for Coca-Cola, and only bought a little pot to smoke recreationally here and there.

When I got to Ted's, his wife started crying, she ran over to me, and hugged and kissed me on my cheek. I was quite shocked with her emotional greeting. I turned to Ted and he gave me a big bear hug. "What's going on?" I asked. They told me they were so glad I was alive. I didn't know what was going on, so I asked them to explain.

We made our way to the living room and they began to explain. Scott had told them that I had stolen the Corvette and taken all the money. According to what Scott told them, Scott and Dale had caught up with me and taken me to an abandoned house. There, they had tied me on the roof in the sun for three days to get me to give them $25,000. They said I had finally broken and given them the money. Then, they supposedly killed me and fed me to the alligators.

At this point, there was no reason to tell them the real story because I had a different plan. We talked about all kinds of normal life items and I asked them to see if Dale and Scott might come over to talk things out. Before he made the call, I asked Ted to not let them know I was there. Ted agreed.

Nobody seemed to be able to get a hold of Scott, but Dale could come. When he arrived, I stayed in the living room out of eyesight but within ear shot. Ted brought Dale into the living room, the look on his face was one of serious fear. With the kids in bed, and the three adults standing in the room, I decided that they deserved to hear the truth. I told them what had really happened. After they heard the true story, all of them knew that Scott had duped them.

I was still pretty angry with Dale for what he had done the day before. I realized he had done it believing his brother. Since he was truly sorry for how things went down, I had to rethink what I wanted to do to him. I walked him into the kitchen and under no certain terms told him that there would never be a second chance with me. He had just spent all his chips. I told him "Don't get in a hurry to leave here tonight, because I will not see you again."

All this over one Corvette and a drunken girl.

32

Mushrooms for a Birthday Party

The Florida weather was turning from hot to sweltering. Summers get miserable there, so when July rolled around I thought it would be nice to make a run to Massachusetts. To cover my expenses, I thought I would pick some silicide mushrooms out of the cow pasture around where I was staying. I figured people would buy enough to get high on and in return put some money in my pocket.

Now most people don't like you walking through their cow pasture for any reason, especially not to pick mushrooms. When picking this type of mushroom you needed to go out early in the morning. The mushrooms sprout up out of the cow manure early and by afternoon, the sun has destroyed most all of them.

I got a couple other guys and made a deal with them to help me pick the mushrooms so we could speed the process up a bit. We each started out with a large paper grocery bag in a pasture that was difficult to see from the road and house. There was a tall tree line around most of the outer perimeter by the fence line on this pasture.

It was a bit slow at first, but it didn't take long to get into the swing of things. Of course, we decided to eat a mushroom or two as we went along picking them. They tasted awful! Wet, slimy, a bit gritty, and growing out of dried up cow dung. Not too appealing to eat if you look where they are growing from. But sooner or later as you're picking, you are bound to eat a mushroom or two. By the time we came out of the pasture, we were higher than a Georgia pine.

We took the mushrooms back to my place where I had an old screen door lain across two sawhorses to dry them. We put as many as we could on the screen door and I told the guys to take all they wanted home with them. I can't say how little or how many they took as we were all tripping pretty hard. Nonetheless, when all was done, I ended up with 13 pounds of mushrooms. That was way more than I thought I would get.

Within a week, we were on our way north to Massachusetts by way of Tennessee. I wanted to sell some of the mushrooms to a few people I knew just north of Chattanooga. This would give me some traveling money. That went off without a hitch and left me with 8 pounds of mushrooms still and plenty of traveling money.

When Pam and I got to Massachusetts, Bobby and Mike with their crew had a couple of deals going down, so I went along as security and made enough money that I no longer had to sell the mushrooms. That turned out to be a good thing too because everybody up there were all a bit scared to try the mushrooms which meant I would have had a rough time trying to sell them.

We decided to have a Fourth of July/birthday party. It was past the Fourth of July and still not anyone's birthday, but Bobby's birthday was in August and I had a birth certificate that said I was born in July, so that was a good enough reason to have a birthday party. We rented a large hall with an open first floor about the size of a basketball court and a full basement of the same size. The first floor was completely open with tables and chairs lining the outer edge. There was a small stage for bands, and in one corner there was a tiny kitchen or serving station. Downstairs there were pool tables, pinball machines, and other games to play.

When we got all the plans made, I offered to help the greeter at the front door. The crowd was going to be a varied but pretty wild bunch. A lot of bikers would be coming. We had invited most of the members from two local clubs and were expecting over 100 people. It was pretty much an open party and almost anyone was invited.

I found three huge, 90-cup coffee urns in the kitchen. Without saying anything to anyone, I took charge of making the punch. We had all kinds of punch drink mix so I mixed some up in a large pot that must of held 3 gallons. I had about 5 pounds of mushrooms left, so I pureed them with a blender I found lying around and threw them into the punch. I half-filled the coffee urns with ice and put the mushroom mix in two of them and regular, untainted punch in the third. I found some pretty small paper cups in a storage room downstairs, they must have held no more than 4 ounces each, so pretty small. I set up the table right inside by the front door and my plan was to give everyone a cup of juice as they entered. The people I needed to keep straight I served from the safe punch urn. Well, it was almost clean. There's a big difference between being high on mushrooms and just a little alcohol buzz.

People started showing up in troves at nightfall. In addition to our guests, there was the regular crowd that always showed up to this venue to party who we didn't really know. As the evening moved on, I was handing out cups of "punch" to everyone that entered. After a couple of hours, you could tell almost everyone was buzzing on something; there were plenty of drugs and alcohol everywhere. And to top it off most had a mushroom buzz that helped them along. Finally, I just put paper signs on the coffee urns saying what was in each one and let them serve themselves.

Outside the back of the hall there was an open field about the size of an acre. The rear steps going out that way had been removed as they were remodeling the back of the building. However, there were some 2 x 12 planks that the bikers set up so they could ride their bikes into the dance hall. The brothers did this with surprising balance while stoned out of their minds.

The party was going well. No fights or even arguments. As I was standing out front on the steps that entered the hall, a lot of people were coming by to talk to me for a minute or two wishing me a happy birthday. That seemed comically odd because none of them even knew who I was and it wasn't really my birthday. This one young couple came over to me and started talking. At first I wasn't paying them much attention, but then they got real serious about giving me a birthday present. At that moment, the girl took off her top to expose her breasts. At that moment, she had my full attention; after all she was quite stunning looking at me with those big doe eyes and perfect breasts exposed to the cool night air. It was their intention that she was to be my birthday present. Now I must admit that was one of the finest offers I ever had on any birthday. But I talked them out of the idea because I knew they'd drunk way too much mushroom punch. I just gave the girl a big hug and a kiss and thanked her very much, then shook hands with her boyfriend or husband, or whatever his relationship to her was, and thanked him. She put her top back on and they walked away and partied on.

Many wild and crazy things happened that night, far too many to write about in detail. One thing though, I remember the cops came by the hall a couple of times. The first time was to remind us that we would have to keep the noise down a bit. I didn't go out to speak to them, Bobby had that honor. I was staying on the edge of the crowd trying not to stick out too much. The second time they came by, the cops had other cars placed on standby just down the road. You see the bike clubs had set some probates in places to watch for anyone coming that they should know about. In turn, we would find out through them that the cops were staged down the road and if a cop car was coming our way. Somebody had fireworks and they decided to set them off all around the outside of the building. It would not have been so bad, but everyone was really wanting a big boom.

So one thing led to another and before any of us knew it, a couple of grenades from who-knows-where were thrown into the large field in back. It was fine because nobody was in harm's way, but the bad thing was there was neighborhood just beyond the clearing. The residents threw a fit and called the cops of course. It had made one heck of a racket in that open field surrounded by trees that were so tall and thick. The echo was deafening. The party-goers had gotten their big boom, the neighbors had been disturbed, and now the cops were coming after us.

Bobby and a couple of his friends talked to the head cop for quite a while as they tried to calm him down. Since they were all locals, they all knew each other, which seemed to work in our favor. Nonetheless, we had to close down the party and get everyone out of there. So that's what we did. It was a birthday party that probably wouldn't be forgotten by anyone who can remember it!

33

First Trip Back to Kansas

After all the birthday party fun, I went back to Florida to check in on things there. Reminded of why I left (the hot Florida mugginess), I decided it was high time I visited Kansas to see if I could reconnect with my family at all. It had been years since I had had any contact with my family whatsoever. This was mid-1981 and I had been gone since 1972. Plus the last time I was there, it had only been for about 24 hours. Prior to that, I left in 1970. It had been almost 11 years since I had talked to or seen any of them. Last I knew, my stepfather Gary was still alive, yet doing poorly with his kidney failure, my brothers and sisters weren't even teenagers, yet except for Betty who was a year older than me.

I thought it would be good for Pam to come along with me to meet my family since I knew all of hers. By this time, Pam and I had a very unusual relationship. She had a vague concept of what I did for a living but had no details of how or what I really did each time I left. Sometimes I would be gone for as long as a month. All she was sure of was that there would be security whenever I was around, and I would make sure that she was taken care of while I was gone. When I told her about going to Kansas to see my family, she was excited to come along. By this time she knew that I was always under an alias name, although I don't think it ever crossed her mind how many identities I was keeping up with. She thought I was only using William Van Sant as my front and everybody just called me Rowdy. Since I didn't let anyone, and I mean anyone, know about my back story, you can bet she was curious about where I really came from and who I really was. This would be the first time that anyone would ever know what my real name was or where I truly originated.

Things were a little strange when we landed in Kansas. Since my Mother had not heard from or seen me in such a long time, neither she nor I was quite sure how to react when I turned up on her doorstep. She seemed a little freaked out, but it was a strange greeting of happiness, sadness, anger, and most of all disbelief. I found out that Gary had passed, and all the rest of my brothers and sisters had grown up and moved out. Then came Mom's confession.

The Feds had staked out Mom's house for such a long period of time and harassed her until she went to the local state representative and ask him to help her get them to leave the family alone. Mom kept telling them that she had no contact with me and didn't know of my whereabouts. The buttheads already knew that because they had Mom's phone tapped and her mail checked. Coming from the small town where we lived, those guys sitting in cars a half-mile from the house was like a neon light screaming, "I'm out of place!" Turns out that the Army had sent a federal arrest warrant out for me back in the early '70s. On paper, I had never completed my full time commitment to the Army and they were collecting. As bad as my PTSD was back then, it turned out I didn't really know what had gone down and how things had happened or what all I had done or not done exactly. But that was long passed now.

Being back in Kansas at this time and place and with the

subject of the Army resurfacing again, I began to suffer from my PTSD really bad. It would get to the point of me blacking out at times and not remembering what I had done in the black out. One of the bad things about the black outs is that I still function and no one knows I am totally out of control. I would go out into the woods away from people at times and then come back out of the black out then wonder what I might have done while out. It took some doing to get it back under control.

Turns out that the Feds never figured out that I was using alias names all around the country. They were looking for some guy named Larry Tannahill, which was me, but it seemed like a life time ago. Nah, Larry Tannahill was a respectable farm boy from the Midwest who worked hard, ran a farm, and watched out for his family. Larry Tannahill was long gone.

A few years after she got these guys to quit watching the house, the military came to her and told her that I was dead. One of my sisters told me that Mom had saved a Christmas present for me in the closet for all those years. That explained why she had been so dumbstruck when I appeared.

When I talked to my brother John, who happened to be visiting home at the time, he told me a story about how he and a friend had been camping in the Colorado woods near a cave. At daybreak one morning of their trip, they found themselves being assaulted by someone but they didn't know who. From the way it went down, it sure sounded like federal agents but we can't be 100 percent. John and his buddy ran inside the cave for cover. Shots were firing around them and they heard their assailants calling my name telling me to come out. John kept hollering to the shooters their names and that I wasn't with them.

They ended up taking the two of them into custody. They released John's friend but took John in for questioning. John and I have a very similar physical build and facial features. The only real distinguishing factor between us is that John has blonde hair and blue eyes and I have brown hair and dark brown eyes. After they were convinced that John was not me they took him out into the woods and dropped him off. If John hadn't been good about knowing how to find his way around and how to survive, he probably wouldn't have made it back out. As he told me all of this, we both agreed that that was their intention. After that, even John thought I was probably dead.
After all the commotion of being reunited with everyone and introducing Pam to my family, we settled down to an uncomfortable situation. No one knew if they really wanted me there or not. It was an awkward pause and no one was sure what was supposed to come next. I decided to go to nearby Fort Riley to see if I could turn myself in to straighten things out with the Army at least.

After talking with the higher ups at Fort Riley for over an hour, they said they'd never heard of me and they didn't have any reason to believe my story or investigate it further. With the military's rejection, I drove back to Mom's place figured I just needed to put a plan together to make some money. I never worried about money, if you know your stuff, money is all around you to be made. So when you need more you set a plan and get to work. It had never failed me yet.

It was a bit strange being back in my hometown. As I went around the two closest towns trying to make contacts and arrangements, everybody kept greeting me as Martin.

John wasn't my only brother who shared my resemblance. Martin, my youngest brother, and I looked pretty similar too and Martin even had the more swarthy complexion like me. John was the only one with an Aryan complexion in the family. Since no one had seen me in almost 11 years, everybody thought I was Martin. This turned out to work in my favor as I wasn't sure I wanted anybody to know I was there anyway. To make this work best, I tried to stay out of direct site or engage in any one-on-one conversations with anybody.

Turns out my little brother Martin was no angel. He had been wheeling and dealing locally for years. Between the two of us we made a deal. He had a few dollars and I knew where I could pick up some Quaaludes in Tennessee. I made up the plan, brought him up to speed, and then I flew off to Tennessee with his backing to pick up a load and fly back.

Just before I left, I didn't know it would be the last time I would be with all of my family: my Brothers and Sisters, Mom, and Grandma. We took pictures on the gravel road just south of the south house that I grew up in.

I got to Tennessee without any problems. It took a few days to settle the deal, so I stayed with Richard and Loretta, a couple I had dealt with many times before. While waiting for everything to be finalized, I went to Chattanooga to spend the night with Loretta's sister and her boyfriend. Her boyfriend was a real piece of crap. We had a mutual dislike for each other so just tried to mind our own business. I'm not going to say why he needed his ass kicked, but he did and probably still does.

34
A Surprise Meeting, A Setup, & A Shootout

Now to one of the best parts of my life. Those few days in Chattanooga created an opportunity for me to meet Katrina. She was a 19-year-old cutie who was staying with my contact's sister. Our group was heading out to party for the evening, so I asked Katrina if she would go with me. She asked me why I wanted her, so I told her I wanted the best looking girl on my arm! That did the trick! She agreed and we went to a bar called Desperados and had a great night.

The next day I was supposed to meet Richard and Loretta to pick up the Quaaludes and have them take me to the airport so I could fly back to Kansas. I met them up in the mountains and we got everything together. It was still about eight hours before flight time, so we took our time getting on our way to the airport. We were stopping to see people that Richard needed to talk to on the way down the mountain. About noon, we stopped in this little diner to get lunch. Loretta was always the motherly type, so after we finished eating she said, "Here: nature vitamins." She gave me what I thought was a vitamin. I just threw it in my mouth and swallowed it with a little bit of water and didn't think anything about it. Little did I know, but it was actually a downer. Anyone who knew me knew that I didn't ever eat downers because they kick my butt. Even a little 5 mg Valium would put me out.

It only took 20 minutes for me to realize that the "nature vitamin" was actually a downer. At first it wasn't too bad and I thought I could hold it together long enough to get past the high to still make my flight. I had been good with Richard and Loretta for a long time and thought they were pretty solid people. In my head I just kept trying to play it off hoping no one else could tell how I was feeling. I was sure it had been an accident. Loretta must have been high herself when she handed it to me.

Before too long we came into a small town named McMinnville. I had to pee something terrible, so we stopped right in the main square of this small town with the courthouse in the middle of the square. While Richard and Loretta went into a small store across the street from the courthouse, I decided to go to the courthouse and use a public bathroom. I was totally wrecked by now and even though I didn't realize it, I was probably stumbling like a damned fool. But I made it to the bathroom.

When I came out of the bathroom there was a policeman there. He said he was gonna lock me up in jail to sober me up so I didn't hurt myself or anybody else. Even though I was higher than a kite, I could still remember what alias name I was running under. It must have worked because they just locked me in a cell overnight to sober up and released me the next morning.
As I mulled over my circumstances from the past 24 hours, I started to piece things together. Richard and Loretta, the downer, the "convenient" stop near the courthouse. They had double-crossed me and turned me in to boot. I don't believe Richard and Loretta thought I would be out the next day. I think they figured once I got arrested and

my history was discovered, I wouldn't get out of jail for a while, if ever! Wrong!

When I got out of jail the next morning, I knew that Richard and Loretta had set me up to swipe the pills I had bought. I guess 10,000 Quaaludes will make people do stupid things. As soon as I got out of jail, I walked to the first car lot and bought an $800 junker. This way I was able to get around to take care of business at least.

I called my brother John in Kansas and told him I had a prepaid ticket at the counter for him to fly to Tennessee. I needed him to bring my brown briefcase. That briefcase had a sawed-off shotgun and a pistol inside. Back in those days you could fly with anything! I gave John the flight number and told him that I would pick him up.

After I picked him up in Chattanooga, we swung by where Katrina lived and picked her up. I'm not exactly sure why or how that worked out, but I'm glad it did because it sure changed my life like it was meant to be. Normally I never would have considered bringing a girl, especially one I cared about, into any kind of trouble – much less a firefight that I would be dishing out. Anyhow, that's just how it worked out. Maybe deep down I was hoping that when Richard and Loretta saw me they would just give me the Quaaludes back and I would be on my way.

There we were, all set in an $800 junk car with my brother John and an innocent 19-year-old girl. I headed up the mountain to Whitey's motel. Whitey was related to Richard and I was pretty sure that's where he would be staying. We pulled into the motel's gravel lot just as it was getting dark. I had gone there with the intention of being in a shoot out if necessary to get back what was mine. I never have been one to tolerate being cheated – especially in such an underhanded way!

I could see Whitey in the door of his office with a pistol in his right hand. I was riding shotgun so I would be able to make full use of that term if need be. As I opened my car door and stepped out, Richard came around the corner of the building with his .30 caliber carbine in hand. So now we were at a standoff. As we all sat there sizing each other up, Katrina slides out of the car not realizing what was about to happen and says to Whitey, "I have to go potty. Can I please use your bathroom?" Now that took all the wind out of what was built up and made us all back down. When she came back from using the facilities, she got in the car and we just drove away. Turns out Katrina's vision wasn't too great at a distance and she had no idea what she'd stepped in the middle of. That whole situation still makes me laugh today.

We swung back by Chattanooga for Katrina to pack a very large suitcase and a whole bunch of other what-have-yous, threw it all in the trunk, and the three of us started driving back to Kansas. That's what I figure you call living life. We were off in car that burned oil like mad with a girl I'd only met days before. I gave up on getting my Quaaludes back or teaching Richard's gang a lesson because they'd only be waiting for me, ready for a shootout. Without the element of surprise of me being out of jail when they thought I was still in jail, I stood no chance to get back anything. I figured it was best to cut our losses and just leave it for the time being.

I started the drive back to Kansas planning to switch back and forth with John as we needed to sleep. After the first stop, we re-fueled with gas and oil then John took over so I could sleep. I slept through another gas stop in which John did not check the oil. As we were rolling along the highway, somewhere in west Tennessee, the car overheated. The motor froze up and there wasn't a thing we could do about it. Now we were stuck on the highway with a girl with too many clothes and a briefcase with a sawed-off shotgun and pistol in it. We had almost no money left and 500 miles to go.

I had Katrina put as much as she could in the one extra large suitcase she had brought. Between John and I it was all we wanted to carry. Then we started hitchhiking to Kansas.

It was hard to get a ride with the three of us. The first ride was from a guy who had just ransacked the car we left behind. He had the new battery I bought back when I got the car. But at least he took us a ways down the road. We walked a lot, got several odd rides here and there, and finally our golden ticket came along. After so long on the road and being almost broke, one last ride picked us up. Even though we were only around St. Louis, Missouri, I knew right then he was going to take us all the way home. I offered to fill up his gas tank as a thank you for the ride. He was pretty okay with that. After I filled the man's car, I bought a bottle of Jack Daniels from the neighboring liquor store. Once we got back out on the road we started drinking. The driver was getting pretty drunk, so I offered to drive. It was a dirty trick I guess, but we felt desperate and the man was all for it in his state of mind. Once I got behind the wheel, I knew we would be home that night for sure.

When our friend with the car sobered up a bit, he realized, more or less, what had happened. But it was too late for him to do anything about it. He was pretty scared that last 100 miles or so. I believe he thought we were going to get rid of him. He was shocked when we got to home. As I pulled in onto the farm property, I drove right up the hill to our 300-gallon gas barrel. I filled his tank to the top, pointed him south on Highway 63, and told him to turn left when he got to Topeka.

Since the deal had gone bad, I had lost Martin all his money. At first I felt pretty bad about that and was trying to figure out what I could do to fix things. But then it turned out that Martin and Pam had been banging each other like rabbits while I was gone. That was the last straw for us. We had already been on the edge of splitting and I don't even know why I thought it was a good idea to bring her to my family's home.

I bought Pam a one-way ticket and sent her back to Florida where $6000 and a car were waiting for her. She had been through a lot with me, and that was my parting gesture and the only way I knew of to bring closure to our relationship and make the best amends I could. Pam eventually remarried and had two children that she could never have had with me. Much later in life, we would be friends and I would meet her children. And that was that. A whole lot of history with someone and time just goes on.

So Martin kept sheepishly avoiding me, scared to death of what I would do to him. That was almost funny though because believe it or not, I wasn't even mad at him. I was just mad over how the deal had gone down and I kept wracking my brain why I hadn't out-maneuvered those scoundrels.

In the meantime, I had Katrina stashed away in my hideout. It was out in the middle of nowhere and she hated it. I got her a little motel room in Wamego, a small town just southwest of the farm. While we were in Wamego, Katrina and I went to a small diner to eat. Our waitress turned out to be my first wife, Marie. By now, I'm not sure what Katrina was thinking! First she's got to be stowed away like some trollop because my wife is at the farm, then we bump into yet another woman who had a history with me! It was starting to look like I was all about one thing! I don't know what Katrina saw in me, but I'm glad she was willing to give me the benefit of the doubt and see where things were going for us. She later said that one of the main reasons she stayed around was because of my "old-fashioned values." You see, I refused to be intimate with her until my divorce was finalized with Pam. That was just the kind of thing that made sense to me. It probably didn't fit in with the rest of the life I was leading, but giving women that kind of respect was one thing that I have always taken very seriously. Plus it just seemed to limit the amount of problems a guy had to deal with if he stuck with that theory.

Anyhow, once Pam left, I brought Katrina to the home place. No more hiding out for her. And I was glad to be rid of the motel bill too.

35

Trip to Florida

After the deal had gone south in Tennessee, it was time to head back to Florida. I needed some traveling money though so it was time to tap into the local resources. Kansas had pot growing all over the place. It was a pest weed that the farmers sprayed with weed killer to keep it under control. There are several different varieties of pot and each has its varying degrees of potency as far as getting a buzz off of it goes. The Kansas weed variety wouldn't really get you high, but it didn't matter. Once it was sprayed with weed killer, it would dry to a golden color earning it the name "Columbian Gold."

Katrina rode with me as I drove through the countryside cutting down lots of sprayed pot and hung it in the garage to dry. Not only did the sprayed pot dry extra fast, but it also looked great. It had nice small, tight buds and both the leaves and buds were perfectly golden. We stripped and bagged it and ended up with three big black garbage bags full of the stuff.

With the pot all finished, it was time to hit the road. I had acquired some kind of green Dodge that towed a trailer with my bike. We packed all kinds of useless junk on the trailer around the bike and the real cargo. Now it looked like we were just moving.

Since Katrina and I had met in Chattanooga, it seemed like as good a place as any to try to dump some of the freshly processed pot. I hooked up with these black guys who lived on the south side of town. That gave us a good point for a quick getaway at least.

When they saw the pot, they fell in love with it. Good color, nice buds! I let them roll a couple of joints to smoke to make sure it was good. Now I knew that crap would not get a fly high, but these boys were high – or least they thought they were! With their approval, they called their moneyman and told him about the sweet goods sitting on their kitchen table. Mr. money was there in less than 30 minutes. He smoked a gold joint and loved it too.

As soon as I heard him say yes, I started to layout the deal for him. After coming to a price agreement on the big bag in front of him, I pocketed the cash and told him I had two more bags on the trailer. He bought it all and now I wanted out of there but quick before someone realized that pot was useless and had no buzz value at all. I walked away with just under $1000 in my pocket. Pretty good for weed-sprayed-gold-pot that I got for free.

All the while, Katrina had been waiting on me, nervous that things would go wrong. The minute I got to the car with a pocket full of money, we hit the road with our sights on South Florida.

As we were driving, I realized that Katrina could hardly see. I kept asking her to describe certain things to me to test out my theory, and she kept failing badly. She needed glasses or contacts or something. When we got to Atlanta I stopped in a mall and we went to find an eyeglass store. Everything went well and she got some contacts. No pretty, young girl wants glasses!

Katrina wanted to know why I had been so generous with buying her the contacts. I told her straight out that it was for if I got shot by someone, she'd be able to describe who they were to me so I would know who to go take care of. I'm not sure she believed me, but I know she loved having the contacts so she could see everything she'd been missing out on in the world around her.

We were coming up on Bradenton so I could finalize things with Pam face-to-face. I couldn't bring Katrina along with me for that, that would have just been asking for it and causing a whole lot of problems. Katrina had a couple of friends who lived over in Pompano on the East Coast, so it seemed best if she flew over there to wait for me and I'd be by in a day or two for her. She gave me the phone number she had for her friends and off she went.

I got everything squared with Pam. She took the car and I kept my bike. Next up was to call the number I had where Katrina was staying. The person who answered the phone wasn't much help and only told me that Katrina wasn't there. So I tried a few more times during the next week or so. I wanted to know the address or whereabouts of where I was going before just heading off blindly. Nothing was working though, so I had no option but to ride over there myself and see if I could find her.

I spent all weekend looking around the Pompano area without any success. I had to get back to the Tampa area to take care of some business, but I rode over to the East Coast every weekend determined to find where I'd sent this poor girl. Fall rolled around, which meant love bug season in Florida. I would run Highway 70 across to 95 and down to Sample road on my motorcycle and get splattered in bug guts. I finally turned up an address of the place Katrina was supposed to be staying, so I went and found the house. Now I knew why the couple was so vague! They were heroin junkies. I found out that Katrina was staying there, but they didn't know where she was at the moment. I gave them a phone number for me, my name, and emphasized how important it was for them to tell her I was looking for her. It turns out they were either too stoned or too stupid to give her my message. Katrina probably figured I had dumped her.

I never bothered going back to the house again after that as junkies just piss me off. But I did keep riding back and forth from the Florida West Coast to the Florida East Coast at least every week. I was sure Katrina still had to be around there.

One day I rode to the Pompano Beach fishing pier looking for Katrina. I parked and decided to stretch my legs by walking out onto the pier. I must've looked pretty out of place compared to all the other beach-goers. I had on leather chaps, a vest, and I was wearing my cowboy boots with one spur. As I walked out onto the pier, I was scanning the shoreline. It was all such a long shot, but maybe she'd be there as much as anywhere I'd been looking. Just then, I thought I saw Katrina sunning in the sand. I hollered her name and sure enough, she looked at me and hollered back. She stood up as I jumped over the rail off the pier down to the sand. We ran together on the beach. It must've been quite a sight, this blonde bikini beauty running into the leather-clad arms of a burly biker. It was better than a movie. She started chattering a mile a minute, the way she does, and I just beamed, knowing all my efforts had paid off. We were reunited at last. We picked up her stuff from the junkies' place and got going back over to the West Coast for me to get my stuff. Even though our plan was to be on the East Coast and down south, neither of us wanted to be separated again!

36

Life in the Glades

Katrina and I settled on Florida's East Coast just fine and were enjoying life. Things were going so good in fact that I invited my brother John to come on out and spend some time with us. He was more than willing to come enjoy the sun and was excited to see me. He had been real young when I had left for Vietnam and we'd never had the chance to get to know each other real well. We were both looking forward to the time together. Katrina and I had quite the operation going in the Everglades just south of Alligator Alley growing pot. It was there that John joined up with us to help work and process the plants.

We had started the pot plants in the early spring so they'd be ready to plant when we did get them down to the glades. All the plants were cuttings off of our best pot plants. This way they were all female plants and when grown, they'd have no seeds in the buds. There is quite a bit to cultivating good pot it turns out. We moved our two small trailers out into the Everglades to live out of. We found a spot and situated the trailers in an L shape, built a porch, and put on a tin roof to protect us from the torrential Florida rain. We screened in the porch because the mosquitoes were so thick.

Our power came from batteries and an old international suburban-type vehicle. All of our lights and fans were 12-volt. We hung a military canvas shower behind the trailer in a tree. We could put water in it to get it warm enough to take a shower.

John and I walked out our path to prep the ground where we would put the plants. We placed them in areas that were hard to get to and not easily noticed. When going out to attend the plants, we never took the same way into or out of the woods. We tried to use game trails as much as possible. We watered, fertilized, and watched our cash crop grow.

Sometimes we would get back to camp and be so covered with mosquitoes that Katrina would spray us down with Yard Guard bug spray through the screen before we could jump in onto the porch. To keep from getting eaten alive, we wore long-sleeved shirts and bush hats with mosquito netting over all the open parts from hat to the shirt. At night the hum from all the mosquitoes on the screen windows of the trailers was deafening.

Don and Judy used to come see us once a month or so to bring supplies. Don had been in the Renegades long before I became one. He and I had many dealings over the years, and were together on this adventure. His wife Judy was good friends with Katrina. On one of these much-appreciated refill trips, Don went back to Bradenton ahead of Judy. Katrina and Judy went to town for something but the car had trouble so the girls got stuck. Judy talked some guy into giving Katrina a ride back to our camp. Katrina didn't want to give our exact location away, so when she thought she was close enough, she had her ride drop her off in the seemingly middle of nowhere. Katrina thought she knew the way, but it became pretty obvious pretty fast that she was lost. She said she just kept trying to make a mental connection with me so I would come and find her, but instead, she was left to cry and fight all the zigzagging dragonflies off on her own. She finally did find it back to camp all on her own. After about hearing the journey, I was just grateful she found the camp before an alligator found her.

Katrina's folks lived in Hollywood, Florida, which isn't that far from the alley on the East Coast. On a supply run into town once, Katrina invited them to come see us in the Glades. "We were living 'back to nature,'" she told them. We had three-wheeler ATVs and we cooked over an open campfire. So when they did come see us we had a great time. We met them on the alley and led them to our camp far off the beaten path. It really looked pretty inviting when you pull up to it. We all rode the three-wheelers around, ate, and had a very fine day.

As the growing season passed, we saw a lot of wildlife in the Glades. One of the most unusual meetings with wildlife came in the dark one night out by our open-air outhouse that was on the edge of the clearing southeast of the trailers. As I was sitting there, I started hearing footsteps coming my direction. From the sound I could not tell if it was one big guy or two. I sat frozen not making a sound. Straining to see into the woods with the very sparse moonlight, I saw movement. As it came out of the woods into the clearing about 15 feet from me, I could make out a large furry creature. There was no question it was a bear. I jumped up and jerked my pants up, which prompted the bear to stand up on his hind legs. Knowing that was the sign of attack, I hollered a couple of choice words and turned for the trailer. As I ran at top speed to towards the porch trailer, I could hear the bear running through the woods in the opposite direction. I'm not sure who was spooked worse, me or the bear. I did see this bear once more as he was crossing the road about 50 yards ahead of me. He didn't look as big in the daylight and that time he was a ways off. He didn't seem to recognize me, but I knew it was him.

Toward the end of our growing season, county maintenance flooded the Glades. The water kept getting deeper and deeper. I'd heard the Everglades were a living river, but we truly saw that in action. The deeper it got, the more we could see the current pulling the water south. We turned on the radio to see if we could find any information about the rising water tables. All we got was some lame water management excuse that didn't seem to make much sense. But then again, government decisions don't have to make sense. All I knew it was time for us to get out while we still could and take toll of the damage later. We couldn't take the vehicles with us, they were already stuck too deep in the mud. On our long walk out, the deer were standing on mud islands and the snakes were everywhere. Some of the snakes were aggressive and I had to shoot a couple to avoid a nasty confrontation. It was an arduous walk in the rising one to three feet of water. After they let the water back down more than a month later we went back to break down the camp. Most all of the pot was lost to root rot from all the water. Time to move on.

37

The Kidnapping

We changed to another position on the East Coast and before long I had started another fine field of pot growing nicely in the middle of the hot Florida sun. We were living out in the middle of nowhere once again. One day I had to go to town for something so I stopped by the stash house to pick up and drop off some things.

When I got there, it was obvious that the house had been compromised. Turns out the family who I rented it to had left their 16-year-old son home while going out. A large black man had forced his way in on the kid and had ransacked the house looking for money or product or both. When he couldn't find anything, he beat the kid up using a tire iron. The kid didn't know anything so finally the man left empty-handed.

After being at the safe house and talking to the family and their son who'd been beaten so badly, I asked them to ride up to the corner store with me so I could buy them some groceries. I knew the family was short on money so I figured the least I could do was treat them and their son to some things. Besides that, a beer or two sounded pretty good after that story to help me clear my head and figure out what I was going to do.

When we pulled into the Circle K parking lot, the 16-year-old suddenly freaked out and ducked down in the front seat of the van. I was in the back by the sliding door watching him and asked him what was wrong. He looked at me and said that the guy in the car next to us was the one who had gotten into the house and beaten him up.

I looked out the window and saw a big black guy sitting in the car. I figured fate had handed me an opportunity. Not wanting to waste it, I opened the van's sliding door, stepped out, yanked the guy's door open, grabbed him, and in one fluid motion pulled him out of his car and threw him into the van closing the door behind us.

By now, my adrenaline was pumping pretty good. I told the 16-year-old's father, who was driving the van "Let's get out of here!" As we drove west out of town, I was giving this guy the lesson of his life. "So! You like to beat up kids huh? Well I like to beat up tough guys!" Since he had used a tire iron on the kid, I thought it was only fair to use an old bumper jack to spank the heck out of him. I let him know in no uncertain terms that he had better never do anything like that again because he would never know when I would be watching him.

As we approached Rye Bridge we started coming up on the several orange groves all around that area. I had the driver stop the van next to a big orange grove on a gravel road. I took the guy out of the van and walked him deep into the grove into a low sloping valley. I put him facedown in the dirt and busted a cap by each ear. I told him this had better remind him not to do anymore dumb shit, like try to rob a safe house and beat up kids. "The ringing in your ears should remind you how close you came to the end," I warned him. That was the last thing I said to him as I left him laying face down in the midst the orange tree roots and headed back to the van.

While I was in the orange grove, there were a couple of kids playing up on the hill. They had seen me pop the caps by the man's head, so they thought I had killed him because he didn't move when I left. They ran home and told their parents what they had just seen. Of course the parents called the cops.

We were about 25 miles from town heading east. All of a sudden, a police car passed us going west. He flipped his lights on, turned around, and sped to catch up with us. The kids must have seen the van too for the cops to have our vehicle description. Turns out it was actually the parents who had seen the van as they drove by on the gravel road when I was out in the grove. With the cop still a ways behind us, I started throwing out my guns: my shotgun, my pistols. You name it I had it, and there it went. The cop didn't stop us, he just followed from quite a long distance behind us. When we came to the first road you could turn off of the highway, the rest of the cops were there to intercept us. They pulled us into a convenience store and the funny part is I was the only one in the car who was worried. Nobody else saw what was wrong with what we'd done. I guess that's because they figured they hadn't done anything. It was all me.

The parking lot was loaded with at least 15 cops and a dozen cop cars. We stepped out of the van, not wanting any trouble, so the cops start separating all of us. Everyone in the van except my brother John had decided I had killed the black man in the orange grove and that's what the others all told the cops.

After the cops were done talking to everyone on the scene, they took me and John to jail and let everyone else go. At least they didn't know John and I were brothers thanks to my alias. Once we got there, they let John go because they didn't have enough evidence to keep him. The only reason they had hauled him along was because he was the only one that didn't say I had killed the man in the orange grove. That was the last time I would ever see my brother John. He left Florida shortly after that, met his would-be wife, Linda, and moved to Massachusetts. He was killed in a motorcycle accident about two years later. I never had the chance to see him in his new life with Linda.

    But back being stuck at the jail. By the time they had finished processing me, they had retrieved the dumbass I had left in the orange grove. They had him at the jail in a wheelchair on this big pillow under his butt. I guess that pussy's ass was too sore from his spanking. I was in handcuffs and the cops were acting pretty smug knowing what they had in store for me. The man in the wheelchair was getting all pumped up with all the cops there blowing smoke up his ass, and trying to line up a good case against me. I had a cop on each side of me with their arms locked through mine so I couldn't move much as I was handcuffed behind my back when that dummy rolled right up to me shooting his mouth off. I just jerked up both legs with the cops holding my arms and dropkicked get that Butthead head over heels wheelchair and all. It felt good.

    That little move earned me a trip upstairs to a 40-man cellblock. As they brought me through the outer gate, the two big black guards announced to all the guys in the cellblock, "This is the guy who kidnapped and beat up the black guy that you saw on the news." Turns out when they opened the second gate, every inmate in there was black except for two young, scared white kids. Great, now they'd just painted it as a hate crime and hung me. I buckled up for a fun time with my new buddies.

    I put my stuff on the only empty bunk and looked around the concrete walls to see whom the main boss of the block was. I saw a massive black dude sitting in front of a chessboard. I walked over to the empty seat at the chessboard and sat down. Before either of us spoke, there had been five or six moves. Conversation was short and small. "So you've played before," he stated as he made a move on the board. I had in fact played before. And not just like a fourth-grader in chess club either. I had learned how to play chess in Vietnam. Tom Richardson was on the 10-minute standby with me and it turned out he played tournaments. I played Tom 75 or so matches before I finally got one on him. All those games were sure paying off now. After I had won three matches from the main boss in the cellblock, he said to me, "You shouldn't have a problem here." We never played again. I didn't want to be seen as any competition to him.

My bail got set for a pretty odd number: $56,000. It would take a while to make that. At least I only had one main problem in the cellblock, which was petty considering the introduction I was given. One day at mealtime, we were lined up at the window to get the chocolate cake they were serving for dessert. One of the small, white boys got a tray with a very large piece of cake. This prick in the line walked up to the kid, slapped him down, and took his tray. I got pissed and grabbed the bully by the hair on his head and his arm and slammed him into the bars on the outer cell wall. His nose and jaw were crooked when he fell to the floor. When the guards came in to get him and find out what happened, the Chess King Boss of the cellblock spoke up and spun some BS story about him falling and that was the end of that.

I finally got bonded after two months, which made me pretty happy because that meant my name and social security number had come back clean. By this time, the Feds had been trying to find me for over six years, maybe longer. The only downside was I had just burnt my most secure ID: William Van Sant. I guess it was for a good cause though.

I met with an old lawyer buddy who used to buy pounds of pot from me. He said my case was a no-win. The best I could hope for was a 17-year plea deal. As a friend, he advised me to disappear or try to make sure no one would testify. I was charged with kidnapping, aggravated battery, and aggravated assault. I spoke to the family whose son had been beaten up and they left for Tennessee within 48 hours of talking to me. John had already split for Utah and the mountains out West. After a few more days, all the players that were with me in the van had gone underground with no way for the cops to find them.

All that was left now was to get a hold of the guy I had kidnapped and pay him off. I contacted Bobby up in Massachusetts and paid his way down so he could try to meet the scumbag and pay him off. I offered $10,000 for him to take a vacation and not come back. That crybaby ran to the cops first thing and told them everything that had happened. This surprised me since he had an arrest record for breaking and entering, robbery, and numerous other things. Nonetheless, that weasel went to the cops and scored 24-hour protection. This significantly diminished my options.

If I didn't show up for my bail hearing, it was like having a bounty out for me from the guy who bonded me – plus he'd get that field of pot that I had been cultivating. The safe house was his already, I was only being paid for protection of the product.

Since Bobby couldn't make the deal, he went back to Massachusetts with some product to cover his expenses and a bit more for a thank you. The bailout man got the pot. I told Katrina to wait for me to see where I would land. I would always come for her, just like in Pompano. I'd have to be on the move from then on and didn't want anyone to know where I would land.

It was time for William Van Sant to officially disappear and for Rowdy to get a new name, date of birth, and all the other documents. I was on my way out of the country. I didn't let anyone know what my name was or where I was planning to go. I rented a car under a different alias to drive to an international airport across the state and then flew out of the country just like that.

38

Off to Jamaica

I had done some smuggling from the Bahamas with some guys named Richie, Wayne, and Mike back before the kidnapping. We had run boats as far south as you can go in the Bahamas picking up loads from Jamaica and points farther south. From the Jamaican connection I had met a bank president from Sava Lamar, Jamaica. So when I flew into Montego Bay, I was going to try and meet up with Mr. Wagstaff, the bank president, and hook up a few flights out loaded with pot.

The Jamaican connection also knew that I grew some of the finest seedless pot (sensimilla) they had ever smoked and they wanted me to look at their operation to see if we could upgrade the quality of product.

With that leverage, I went through Montego Bay customs with no problems. My idea was working perfectly. I was now Robert James Harold born May 10, 1950. I checked into the hotel named the Upper Deck on the side of a hill on the edge of Montego Bay. There I waited for a contact to bring me more information. Before the end of the day, Mr. Wagstaff sent someone to pick me up and get me out of Montego Bay. He had a place for me in Belmont on Bluefield Beach in the West Moreland district.

It was a beautiful part of the island. It wasn't a bustling hub or tourist spot, but rather a quiet, smaller, sprawling village set along Jamaica's west coast. It was upscale without being frivolous and just a clean neighborhood. It was a place where no one would ask any questions. If you lived there, the locals, authorities, and anyone else figured it was because you wanted to and you could. It was the perfect place for me since I was never big on people asking me anything about my business.

There I spent some time with his crew drying, stripping, and packing pot to be shipped out. We used a kitchen garbage compactor to press the pot into square bags then double-wrapped it and taped the bags for transport.

39

Pros and Cons

My old partner, Don, wanted to come to Jamaica for a load of pot. He only had a single-engine plane with visual flight training. This seemed like an ideal way to get Katrina down to Jamaica. I was pretty excited for the deal and we got it all set and in progress. Don could only fly in daylight hours, so they had to stop overnight somewhere along the way. At long last, they finally made it to Montego Bay.

When they arrived they were surprised to see how fast the locals wanted their Styrofoam coolers. You see there is not a lot of refrigeration in the rural areas and any kind of cooler is worth a lot. So this was their first taste of the people in Jamaica. Even after I explained why they wanted their coolers it was hard for them to understand. The culture shock of coming to a developing nation from a first-world country takes some time to grasp. They had never been in another country so they thought everyone had the same advantages that you might have in the United States. And in Jamaica, there are no corner stores selling Styrofoam coolers like you could find on almost city corner at home.

I didn't meet them as they arrived because I would be sending a load home with them in a couple of days and didn't want to draw any extra attention to their arrival. Instead, I met everyone at the Upper Deck after they had checked in at the hotel. I was glad to see Katrina since I had already been in Jamaica a while without her. Life just wasn't the same without her by my side. We all talked and made plans for the next few days.

I spent that whole night with a crew stripping and packing pot into watertight blocks. It was quite a process, but our cargo was too precious not to handle properly. Once the load was ready, we got a drum full of fuel from the airport and smuggled it up on top of the mountain where we had the pot staged. Everything was ready just as daylight was coming on. We just waited for Don to bring his plane by to get it loaded and sent out.

Since the military still did regular fly-overs looking for smugglers, the plane needed to get out just at dawn and we needed to be out of sight in the trees. Our mountain airfield was disguised as a cow pasture, but too many people hanging around would blow that cover real quick. In fact, just a few weeks prior, the military had come up and blown holes in the "pasture" so it couldn't be used to fly in or out. Luckily, the landowner had a tractor and a blade hidden so when the government did their thing he could have the airfield ready for action within a few days again.

As you can see, Jamaican-grown pot was no cheap endeavor. First the field of pot itself, then workers to harvest, set, dry, strip and pack it. All these people had to be paid. Fuel from the airport was a huge expense too. It came at a premium thanks to the airport personnel payoff. The landowner expected compensation as well, and of course the man at the airport with the fake flight plan. It was quite the process and everything had to be precisely calculated.

Don took off from the Montego Bay airport and was a bit nervous landing on the mountain airstrip. It was an expected nervousness for a first-timer. Once he landed, we got the plane turned around, and then we swung into action. My crew scurried to top the fuel off, calculate how many pounds he could carry and still be able to take flight, loaded it all up and then wave him off. The whole process only took a few minutes. We gave him the thumbs up and he started down the runway.

As he went down the runway trying to accumulate enough ground speed, he hit a couple of cow paths and started to take false flight. Instead of keeping her on the ground to get the ground speed up, he tried to take flight. That bad move caused him to stall and crash the plane off to the left side of the airstrip. Now we had a problem! We got him and his co-pilot out of the plane and on their way to get checked out at the hospital. We unloaded the pot, pumped out as much fuel as possible back into the 55-gallon drum we had taken it out of, pulled all the instruments out of the airplane along with anything else that looked valuable. Then it was up to the crew to used whatever they could find to make a chop job out of the plane. We needed all evidence of the entire incident wiped out or else the government would be all over the place. Once the plane was broken down into small enough chunks to handle, we tossed them into the bottom of the ravine and covered it with dirt and brush.

Meantime, the girls, Katrina and Judy, were at the Upper Deck in Montego Bay still waiting for us to get back. I guess Don and his co-pilot Mike went by there to let them know what happened before going to get patched up at the hospital. By the time I got to the Upper Deck it was getting dark. Busy day at the office.

I was up in the room with the girls when the cops arrived. They had gotten wind of the crash somehow but only figured on a pilot and co-pilot and a couple of girls associated with them. They didn't know I was involved, so they told me to get out when I told them I was just trying to hook up with the girls. As the cops took the girls off to be questioned to see what they knew, I went down by the pool and sat in a lounge chair since I didn't have a room key. I felt bad for the girls knowing that the cops were actually looking for me yet they'd taken them and let me walk right out since my story didn't fit with what they were chasing.

The cops gave the girls a hard time to say the least. They were loading them up with rum to get them drunk so they'd talk. They peppered Judy with all kinds of questions trying to get a physical description of her man out of her. She was so drunk she just made goofy hand gestures and talked nonsense. Poor Katrina kept falling apart under the influence of all the booze and pressure, so they called her "cry cry."

It seemed like they kept the girls for a long time so I started walking around. I was beginning to feel a little obvious just hanging by the pool in street clothes by myself. I finally saw the girls walking down a road heading back to the Upper Deck. At least they had been released. I heard all about their interrogation, which was pretty heavy for them to go through. I was sure happy they were with me again, yet I knew from the questions they had been asked it was time to get out of sight. Now that I had Katrina with me in Jamaica I was ready to get back over to the safe house in Belmont where I was staying.

Don, Mike, and Judy got a commercial flight back to the States. The cops heavily questioned them before they left. I don't know what kind of answers they gave, especially with Katrina not returning with them. The bottom line was they didn't know where I was, they didn't know where the airfield was, they just really didn't know anything.

40

Island Living

The house that they had set me up in was on the west side of the island. It was a large house and another couple lived in the other half of the house on the property it was like a U-shaped duplex. Our neighbors were nice quiet people. He was retired Navy and working in the local hospital as an x-ray technician and I don't remember what his wife did. They didn't ask any questions and in return I asked no questions of them.

Anyway we had a cook and maid who came with the house, and Dion our runner. He was a young boy, maybe 13 or 14, who would help us find things or go get them when we needed them. We lived at this place for quite some time. At the back of the house was a pier that went about 50-60 feet out into the water. It was great. I used to go spearfishing a lot and the cook for the house would make a meal for myself and her family. See we had a gas stove and she didn't have a stove at all in her home. So she always had food to take home because Katrina didn't eat fish. The cook was always trying to give me pot in hopes I would want some, get hooked, and then buy from her so she could make a little extra on the side. I don't think she ever really figured out what I was doing. Between the police chief of Petersfield and the head banker from Sava Lamar, I'm sure she was pretty confused about my existence there.

Dion was a great kid. He Helped us find anything and everything we needed. He had a bicycle so he made short work of getting things from downtown or anywhere else. He was a great help. For Christmas I went over to Dion's family's house and helped him paint the house for his Mom. I think it really surprised him that I was willing to do that with him.

Mr. Wagstaff also invited us over to his house for Christmas. We had curry goat and some homemade drink. We thoroughly enjoyed our time with them learning about the culture and way of life on the island.

Then there was Katie's Keg. It was the local bar just down the road from where we lived. They served warm beer, played good reggae music, and everyone treated Katrina and I great. We almost felt like celebrities living the good life amongst the friendly Jamaicans.

Then things started getting hot on me. I had been exchanging money from US to Jamaican. I was getting a great rate of exchange on the black market in those days: $20 Jamaican for $1 US dollar. It got so bad that my driver would have to let me hide in the trunk so I wouldn't be seen. Every time the cops would see me riding with someone, they'd stop us and ask for "lunch money." I'd have to give them money so we could be on our way.

The people I was working with were also growing fields of pot up in the mountains. They wanted me to see their operation so I went to the mountain to see their fields of pot and check out how they were growing. We picked up two coolers, filled them with ice and red stripe beer and drove as far up the mountain as we could. Then we walked the rest of the way carrying the coolers. When we got to the camp, the crew was very happy to see us as they rarely had visitors. As soon as they realized we had brought ice they took all the beer out and butchered the goat that they had been raising up there and put him on ice to cool.

That night they cooked the goat with beans and made spinners, which were a dumpling dough they'd roll between their hands and drop them into the pot to cook. We smoked pot wrapped in old grocery sacks for papers because none of us had any rolling paper. We washed it down with the hot red striped beer while we talked about growing pot of the best quality possible. The Jamaican mountains are pretty much wall-to-wall pot fields. There was an imaginary line strung from the top of the mountain to the bottom marking the dividing line between fields. With so much pot grown in the same area, there was no way they could grow seedless pot. There were too many different farmers up there growing their own fields and to grow seedless pot all the growers would've had to be in on it. Anyway, I came off the mountain full of good food, buzzed from warm beer, and had a definite sore throat from smoking pot rolled in a brown grocery sack.

After we'd been in Jamaica about six months, our friends Richie and Priscilla were planning to come down to put a load together. I had done some smuggling with Richie before and was looking forward to seeing my pal. They tracked us down by asking around. It's funny in a way because all those folks knew us just as Rowdy and Katrina. None of them ever knew about all of my aliases or that I went south because of the kidnapping. They just knew we could all do some business.

41

Aiming for Nassau, Back to Kingston

Richie left with his load and Priscilla stayed behind to keep Katrina company while I went on another business venture to Nassau in the Bahamas. The girls would come my way on their own in a few days. You see neither of them was on the lam and I didn't want anyone with me if things went wrong.

My plan was to fly from Montego Bay to Miami with a flight change from Miami to Nassau. That way I would not have to go through customs. As things went, I arrived in Miami with no problem. I was standing in line to get my boarding pass to fly from Miami to Nassau when from somewhere behind me I heard someone call out, "Hi Rowdy!" As the person called my name the second time, my blood was running cold. What were the odds that someone would know me in this ticket line, and of course while I was using my alias?

Not wanting to draw any more attention to myself, I turned to see who it was. It turned out to be someone who had worked deals with me from long before who we all just called Tuna. I relaxed a bit after that, but I didn't want him hollering my name out again. I avoided this by getting out of line, walking back to him, and going through the boarding pass line behind him. That way he could have his pass and be out of the way before I showed the ticket agent my ID with a name I didn't want him to see. That was a close one. I always tried to keep my IDs straight and never cross multiple IDs to anyone.

On the flight to Nassau, Tuna told me about needing some help with a planeload of pot down in Kingston, Jamaica. The load was paid for and just needed to be moved. We came to an agreement that I would fly down with the Jamaican man who had done the deal and make sure everything was set up right. When we got to Nassau we went to his room at the casino. He called the Jamaican to set it up to meet me in Miami where the two of us had met earlier. This way, I wouldn't have to go through customs and he would have already cleared through. He gave me money to make the trip, rent a car, and walking money so I was off again, right back to Montego Bay via Miami again.

The load of pot that I was going to Nassau for would have to wait. If it couldn't be rescheduled then it would go down without me. This also changed Katrina's plans. She would now fly back to the States with Richie's girlfriend, as she had no idea I was going back to Jamaica. Sometimes it's just best that you don't let anyone know what you're up to so they don't have a reason to worry. This was for sure one of those times.

My contact in Miami said he was Jamaican and gave me some name that I can't even remember. On the flight down to Jamaica we sat on different parts of the plane. I didn't want to be too close to this guy, I got an uneasy feeling about him. After doing that type of work for as long as I had, I'd learned it was best to trust your gut. When you don't, you can make mistakes that will cost you.

We arrived in Montego Bay and rendezvoused outside the airport. The first order of business was to rent a car and head for Kingston. I had him rent it with his driver's license since he was the native Jamaican and of course it made more sense for him to drive the roads he would have been slightly more familiar with than me. We got into the car and as we pulled out of the rental lot, there was a round about right there. He got into the wrong lane, and went the wrong way around the roundabout, which was a dead giveaway that he wasn't a Jamaican or else he would have known to drive on the left side of the road. Before we could get killed, I yelled at him to pull over and stop. I told him to get out and I would drive so we wouldn't die. We switched places and were off again. In those first couple of minutes I had learn a lot. First he was not from Jamaica and didn't even know how to drive on the left side of the road. Second that he was lying to me.

As I drove us to our destination, he told me about the twin-engine plane that was sitting on the airfield in Kingston. I drove us straight to the airport to check the plane and the load. When we got to the private plane section of the airport, I pulled up to the chain-link fence to go through the gate. All of a sudden, he got real nervous and said to me "don't pull in they will see us." I stopped and parked by the fence in stead. I asked him how in the hell we were supposed to check things out if we couldn't go out to the plane? He told me we should go see the guy that owns the plane and he could take us out there to see it. The information I had was that the $15,000 had already been paid for the load and they just needed a pilot to fly it home. But with all the conflicting stories and white lies popping up, I was mentally scrambling to figure out exactly what I was into. All I knew was I had to go along with things to a certain point and I wouldn't know when the "get out" point was until I felt it.

The guy guided me to a trailer park on the outskirts of Kingston. I could tell he had been there before. But that made things even stranger. He couldn't drive, yet he knew his way around that part of Kingston. When we got close to the house that he needed to go to he had me stop short by a hundred feet or so. He said, "Come on let's go in and see the man." There was no way I was walking into an unknown situation like that. I told him he'd have to bring the men out to meet me. After some disagreement and discussion he agreed.

Once he disappeared into the house, I turned the car around facing toward the exit of the trailer park. The hair on the back of my neck was standing up so I knew things were about to get bad. In the rearview mirror I saw my "partner" running toward the car with two guys chasing him with machetes. I started the car, opened the door, and took off just as he jumped in. Two gunshots rang out with one bullet hitting the back of the car.

After we were safely away, I found a place to stop on the side of road. By now, the guy was scared to death. I'm not sure who he was more worried about: the guys who had chased him or me. At that moment I was making sure he was scared to death of me. I made it clear to him that I would deliver him back to the machete boys one way or another if I didn't get some honest answers.

He spilled everything. He had already done a load with these guys but hadn't paid them. He told them he was bringing the man with the money down to meet them. I was supposed to be the money man. When we got to the house without the money, they were going to kill both of us. There was no plane, no load, only a set up to kill me for non-payment of a load I knew nothing about! I was pissed now. I threw the butthead out of the car, gave him a proper ass whipping, got back in the car and drove to Montego Bay. I just left the car at the airport. It was in his name not mine after all. I got on the plane for Miami and back on to Nassau.

In the end I found out that Tuna had put up money to initiate the original deal. Since he didn't go himself or send someone he trusted to watch out for his interest, this knot head used Tuna's money for something else. So the knot head sold Tuna this excuse about the load just needing to be flown back. I am not totally clear on just how much trouble or what for sure he had told the people in Jamaica. From the look in their eyes and the ease with which I was shot at, I do believe his story about them fronting him a load of pot that he never paid for and me acting as the stage money man. I'm sure there was more to the story, but I'm happy I got out when I did and never found out the rest.

42

Nassau at Last

The Kingston fiasco had made me two days late to Nassau so my contact wasn't there. In fact, I was all but broke and had no way to contact anyone to get any money sent. Besides, I'd come to do some work of a questionable nature, so I didn't want to draw any attention to myself.

I decided to camp out on the east end of Nassau by the harbor inlet where there was an old fort. I spent my days there and my nights in the abandoned hotel across the road called the Montague Hotel. The Montague was one of Al Capone's places to bring in rum in times long past. The rumor was that even John Kennedy senior might have had a run or two through there. Funny thinking how now I had free run of the joint. Of course it wasn't in near the same condition, but it was interesting to think about nonetheless. The light tower on top must've been four stories high. That's where they signaled the ships to come in or to hold out.

I knew that sooner or later the people I was supposed to meet up with would approach me. On my second day there, a man came to speak to me briefly and told me to contact his friend. I sat on the information for a couple days until he came by again. This time, he repeated the message and handed me $200. Now that I knew he was serious, I called the guy who wanted me to go to Nassau to let him know I had made contact. With some money finally in hand, I rented a cheap room, took a shower, and bought some food. Once I had been confirmed as the right guy, Brett (the $200 man), found me and put me up in a house on the third floor.

I did a few small jobs for Brett while the first month or so passed. I made a couple of connections that helped me get hooked up tight into a local crew. The business was changing from all pot to pot and cocaine. Cocaine was smaller packages and more money. After I had some buyers fly down from Boston in their jet and make a nice buy, I was in with all involved on this end.

I got an apartment to live in paid for by whomever. Nobody told me exactly who paid the bills and I didn't ask. I was the guard, protector, or enforcer whatever they needed. I started working on a 42-foot Grand Banks trawler. I spent most every day that I could working on her. During this time I, finally felt secure enough to have Katrina fly to Nassau to be with me. We had some good times there. The best burgers were from a little place called La Shack. It was close to where we lived so we went there often.

Ever since Katrina and I hooked up, she travelled with me to all kinds of places. It was a very different relationship than I'd ever been in before, and I have to say I sure liked it. I still tried my best not to let her get into any tight spots on my account. That worked out most of the time. When I would go to different states or countries, I would go ahead and then she would wait for my call to have her come meet me.

She could make friends anywhere and pretty much talk to

anyone. That skill of hers was great since I didn't have that much talk for most people and she could keep a roomful entertained without any focus being put on me. But she wasn't just a diversion from my high-risk, underworld life. I liked having her with me. She was closer to me than anyone had ever been in my entire life.

I don't think she thought too much about my lifestyle at first: "It's just what I did." As time wore on and she understood the reality of what I was tied up in, my business would bother her more. I know there were times when she worried and fretted and even feared for me, but she accepted me for who and what I was. She also knew that no matter what I would protect her and take care of her. She was my number one priority, my everything. The rest was just work.

    I don't believe she ever felt that she was living on the edge because she was never directly involved in anything. As for me, it was just normal so she never had to feel uneasy about things because I didn't project that. Our life appeared to be normal to all who didn't really know us. And that was pretty much everyone.

43

The Bahamas Life

There was a nightclub close by frequented mostly locals. Katrina and I would walk there and spend time drinking and then walk home. One night as we were walking home, this car rolled up beside us. A guy jumped out and hit me in the head with a large rock. He fully expected me to go down, but all he did was piss me off. Since I hadn't dropped as planned, two more guys got out of the car. As I scrapped with rock hitter trying to get a hold of him, he slipped back into their car trying to hurry and get the door closed. Since he was giving up, the other two who had jumped out, the driver and front seat passenger decided they'd better bail too. They jumped back in the car but not before I could grab the same rock that had been used on me. As the car pulled away, I hurled the rock right through the window hitting the guy who had first hit me. They ran like chickens!

I was never sure why they did it. Could be that they wanted to rob us or maybe they were going to try and kidnap Katrina. I often wonder what their motive was. Whatever it was, it was squashed. My souvenir from the incident was a fairly large knot on my forehead that kept haunting me for days.

The next morning I had a job to do. Three of us had to go to Andro's Island to do a bit of business. On the way back to Nassau, a storm blew in on us. We were in a 26-foot open fisherman and it got rough. At one point the waves were 7 to 10 feet tall. I banged my head on one of the Bimini top rails. It was so rough at times that our feet were 2 feet above the deck as we were bounced into the air. It turned our normal 20-minutre return trip into a two-hours struggle. It was sure good to have that one behind us, but my head was sure ready for a break.

As the rock incident proved, Nassau was a pretty rugged place in a lot of parts. But then there was the high-end side of the island. The side that all the celebrities and foofy-fancy folks escaped to.

Gray Cliff was a restaurant, maybe the fanciest restaurant, on Nassau. It was the kind of place you had to have a jacket to eat at. (By the way I borrowed one.) This was one of Mick Jagger's places to frequent. He had a house right down the street on the island. It was the big time.

It was Valentine's Day so Brent, Liliana, Katrina, and I all went together. Brent picked out the place since he was a native and knew the chef. The chef came to our table and said he would cook us a special meal. First he talked to us to find out our likes and he took it from there. We had a fantastic custom meal and two bottles of wine. I believe the two bottles came to 1200 bucks and the meal was a couple hundred dollars apiece. When we left, our bill, with the tip, came to $2600!

That was the most expensive meal I've ever had. I felt a bit odd. There I was in a borrowed jacket with a big bandage on my forehead from when I had been hit it in the head with that rock. We paid

$10 for a Polaroid picture while sitting at the table to boot. Turned out to be a fine time all-in-all.

Our little crew decided we needed some down time so Brett, Liliana, Katrina, another couple, and I went to one of the outer islands. It was a short trip, so we just rode out in a small whaler with a single outboard engine. The trip over was nice and smooth and we all had a great time there. We goofed around in the shallow water, the girls went topless to get some sun, the guys hunted for conch to make proper conch salad. It was a nice time.

We started back north by northwest toward Nassau and for the first half of the trip all went well. Then we started having engine problems. Brett hadn't put a tool bag on board so when the engine died, we were adrift.

After quite some time we were spotted by the island shell tanker. This was the tanker that would haul fuel throughout the islands. They pulled alongside and gave us some fresh fuel. They also loaned us a wrench so we could clean the spark plug. After some time, we got the engine started. We thanked the guys on the tanker and headed on toward Nassau. As we got closer, we could see the Montague Hotel and knew we were close enough that we would make it. The trip that we started out just to have fun on turned out to be a real pain in the neck. But at least we got back on shore and everything turned out all right. Thank goodness that tanker had spotted us and been nice enough to help us out.

44
Losing it All

During this whole time, I was still getting that 42-foot Grand Banks boat cleaned up and ready to use. That time was about to arrive. It was time to set up for a full run. We had gotten a hold of Frank, an airplane pilot in Oklahoma, and arranged for him to buy a plane. He picked up an above-winged plane, which would make our drops easier. With an above-winged plane, you could open the doors and throw the load out into the ocean without any obstructions. Then he would simply fly the plane back to Nassau. Not having to make landfall would make most transactions a lot easier.

In the meantime, a boat smuggler named Mike came over from the States in a 30-foot Ocean Master. It was a very nice open freshman-style boat with a wide beam and twin outboards. The wide beam made it a very dry boat to run because it would throw the water outwards away from the boat as it broke through the waves. Pretty nice feature really.

I had done a couple of runs in it before. Like when Mike and I had picked up a 2500-pound load of pot. Long before I had gone to

Jamaica, Mike and I had made a few quick, short runs together. We had picked this load up at Andros Island in the Bahamas. The boat was loaded to the gunwales and we needed fuel so we pulled into Bimini. It was late and very dark so we pulled right up to the fuel dock. Mike went to pay and I got ready to pump. All went well. The dock master didn't even come close to the boat. Of course he knew what was happening and didn't want any involvement. He also knew what was waiting on the outside of the West Inlet if he objected to our refueling needs. I guess he had a "smuggle at your own risk" policy.

After we fueled and started west out the inlet, we knew there was a sandbar that would make us turn south to get around it before taking our heading for West Palm Beach. As we came out and started south, we met up with a 119-foot Coast Guard ship with all his lights on and shining everywhere. We were close enough to see everyone clearly, so we knew they could see us no problem. Not sure exactly what to do, we waved to them and they waved back. Always better to be polite and friendly. As we came around the sand bar we tried to stay just on the outer edge of the lights from the ship. We keep our speed down as not to raise any suspicion until we were well away from the ship. We did some moves to act like we were fishing in case we were on their radar. All went well and we completed the run just like that.

As we met up in Nassau this time to make this trip, we were hoping for a repeat smooth trip this time around too. We had put together quite the load. Frank was a helicopter pilot in Vietnam, so he made a good smuggling pilot. He had a good head on his shoulders and did not lose his nerve in a tight spot. He and his co-pilot would be the ones to go to Columbia and pick up the load.

While they were on their way to Columbia, Mike and I would take the Grand Banks to Spanish Wales and Brett would bring the

Ocean Master. The Grand Banks was a very slow boat so we would leave way ahead of the Ocean Master. We would also carry all the extra equipment with us. We had our own ADF transponder so the plane could find us and set up his drop to us. Then the 30-foot would pick up the dropped load and bring it to the Grand Banks and we would slowly bring it home. It seemed like an easy enough basic plan.

We all stayed away from each other most of the time leading up to the run so we wouldn't draw any suspicion to ourselves in case any of us were being watched. When we would meet, we were never all in one place together for longer than anyone would casually meet someone they knew.

Once we were set, everything went into motion. Frank and his co-pilot flew to Columbia. Mike and I prepped and fueled both boats. This would be a night drop to have better cover. My job, other than helping all around, was to be the guard. We had to protect our load from pirates. Yes, pirates! On the high seas whoever has the most firepower or best shot is the one who ends up with the load.

For a night drop you need glow sticks for the bails so you can find them. That would be the co-pilot's duty before he threw the bails out. The ADF transponder was so the pilot could line up the plane on the boat to make a direct drop. We also needed radios so we could talk to the pilot when he flew within range. The Grand Banks had a satellite navigation system to give exact location to the pilot also. After all, you didn't want them to drop a bail of pot through the deck of the boat.

As Frank was down in Columbia loading, we were on our way to the drop zone. On our way to Spanish Wales, a storm blew in. This was bad news as the Grand Banks was like a floating cork and slow even on calm seas. As we got closer to our mark it was well into the night with rain and big waves. It was so dark you couldn't see much of anything. Brett was ahead of us and called us on the radio to ask if we could see the lighthouse. Mike told him we could, but we didn't know if we were clear of all the rocks before the channel to the north. He said he could see us and our lights bobbing up and down and that he had just come through the channel and for us to turn and head for the lighthouse. We could not see Brett or the 30-foot boat because he only had running lights on. We were much easier to see with our cabin lights, tower lights, and running lights al flared up. We made the mistake of turning to the light on the lighthouse like Brett said. After all, he was the owner the Grand Banks.

We turned and no more than two or three minutes later, the waves suddenly stopped bouncing us around and we hit something hard. It was so hard that it threw Mike up on the console and almost threw me to the deck. Mike put the motors in neutral and I grabbed a flashlight to go see what we had hit. I opened the cabin door and started forward toward the bow on the starboard side. I was not ready for what I was about to see. We had struck an enormous rock formation about 4 feet high and 25 feet long jutting up out of the water. I shone my light down on the starboard bow and there was a hole the size of a basketball below the waterline. I ran back to the cabin and opened the engine doors then jumped down inside to see if I could pump out enough water to keep us afloat.

It was no use. The water started to come over the top of the front cabin door into the engine room. The bow of the boat was going down. The cabin door gave way and swung open. In that moment, I went from knee-deep water to neck deep water. I swam out of the engine room to get to the deck mid-ship starboard side. I looked around and knew there was no saving any of the equipment.

I got to the stern of the boat where Mike was trying to get the towrope to the dinghy untangled from around the prop. It had tangled when we had hit with such force before Mike was able to get the engines into neutral. Now the dinghy was pulled up tight to the stern of the boat. While the bow was going underwater and the stern was completely out of the water pulling the whaler up with it. I had a knife so I crawled over to the stern while Mike held the light and I cut the tow rope away. The dinghy fell back into the water and I jumped for it. There was no rope to hold onto it with and I was afraid it would float away, so it was the only means to our survival. I grabbed a hold of the prop and Mike jumped into the whaler. All this time the Grand Banks was sinking into the water.

We were in the dinghy and Mike was trying to get it started as the Grand Banks completely submerged. The water was only around 20-feet deep where we had bounced off the rock. As she lay on the bottom with all her lights still on, it looked odd to me. She was still alive but empty.

We finally got the outboard motor started but now we were in another fix. We couldn't see anything because of the rain coupled with the darkness. Any moonlight that would have been out was obscured by fearsome rain clouds. All we had was a flashlight to try to find a way to somewhere safe. Mike had managed to grab one of the handheld radios on board. He was able to call Brent with it to let him know what was happening. Even though he couldn't find us because he couldn't see us in the storm, at least he knew we were alive. Mike was at the helm and I manned the bow shining the puny flashlight beam into the relentless dark searching for something, anywhere safe. After what seemed like hours, we found a sandy beach to pull the dinghy up on and breathed a sigh of relief. We could wait out the night in some peace knowing we had reached land of some kind.

That gave us time to think. We realized how bad things were all around. It was storming like nobody's business and Frank was still on the way with the load. We lost the ADF transponder in the Grand Banks so we had no way to line them up or bring them in to drop the load. He couldn't see the spotlight on the 30-foot because of the storm. But we did have contact with him through the radios up until almost daylight. He was flying around looking for us but had to give up and try to find a safe landing zone because he was running low on fuel. As daylight came, Brett found us on a sandy little spit of an island. We tied the whaler to the 30-foot Ocean Master and headed back to Nassau. We were worried about Frank, the co-pilot, the plane, and the load. We did not know if anything had happened to them or what.

When we got back to my place in Nassau and no one had heard from Frank, we set a search team in motion for him. We sent out three smaller planes to cover the area where we last knew of his location. We waited for news from someone or anyone. It finally came late in the afternoon. Frank called from Freeport. He and his co-pilot were alive. The police had questioned them and now they were going to leave for the States on the next flight out.

We finally found out the rest of their side of the story too. They hadn't heard us clearly on the radio about what was going on with us in the water. They did understand that the ADF was lost and that they couldn't have a true location on us. They were flying around the area hoping for a break in the weather to try and see us. As the storm was clearing up and the sun was rising, they were running out of fuel. They had to make the critical call to land laden with illegal drugs, or bail. They saw a cruise ship close by, so they put their life vests on, grabbed the hatchet, and flew over the bow of the cruise ship very low so everyone could see them.

The cruise ship couldn't stop in time to pick them up. By the time they belly landed the plane in the water and chopped the window out with the hatchet to get free of the plane, the ship was too far away. They landed in the water that was just over the shallow ledge in 700 foot of deep water. They were too far from any land to swim to shore. Luckily, the cruise ship had radioed to a freighter that was behind them in the shipping lane to let them know there were two men in the water ahead of them.

When the freighter got close to them, they shot a life raft off the bow toward them. The wind caught the life raft and set in sailing back over the ship on the opposite side, so that attempt failed. The second shot proved to be a success and they pulled them both to the safety of the ship. After having been in the water for four hours, they were in rough shape. By the time the freighter stopped in Freeport they were all right.

The police questioned them knowing that they were probably smugglers, but no plane, no pot so what could they do? The other problem was there was no flight plan from anywhere. In the end, they just told them to go back to the States and stay there.

Everything was a bust. We lost the plane that had just been bought. It hadn't even had a chance to pay for itself. We lost the 800 pounds of pot that had just been bought. We lost the 42-foot Grand Banks that I had just spent the last three months priming to make this trip.

There was no way we could just leave the Grand Banks there. Everyone knew who owned it and that I had been working on it. We had to hire a recovery team to fish it out and get rid of it for good. The recovery team got to keep the boat and all that was on it rather than write a report about it. This way they kept quiet even though they could tell what the boat had been rigged for.

Even though we lost all that equipment and dope, we considered ourselves still in good shape. We didn't lose anyone. There's always another plane or boat and always another load. It's the people who do what we did that we could never replace. Good solid crews are far and few between.

45

A Vacation to Remember

I had just done a run and made a pocketful of money, so Katrina and I decided to fly some people over to the islands. We wanted to give them a vacation they would always remember. Katrina and I came up with this idea as we rode our little motorcycle around Nassau. The little motorcycle was a great way to get around the island! Before we had it, it was all walking. Turns out it was good for brainstorming too.

We flew Pam and Jackie and Danny over from the States. Mine and Pam's divorce had been finalized for quite some time and fortunately we all still got along – including Katrina. We had a great time playing tourists alongside them and doing all the sightseeing things. It was good to just relax and enjoy life together.

Shortly before it was time for everyone to fly back home, we spent a night in the Grand Hotel on Paradise Island. Nobody else knew that I would be returning from my self-imposed exile too. I had secured a new name and Social Security number through various means and I was feeling ready to leave behind the Caribbean life and get back to the US. My new identity would be Robert James Harold. I was sure it wouldn't raise any red flags traveling through customs and all. I would just need to fly under the radar once I returned to "normal" living. My plan was to settle down in North Carolina since I hadn't been all over that state yet. Tennessee, Massachusetts, Florida, Kansas, and Missouri were all ruled out due to my history in those states. I just couldn't risk it.

Maybe I was excited to have visitors or maybe I was excited about my upcoming prospects of returning to the States. Whatever it was, I just kept drinking. That night I bought every bottle of Dom Perignon the Grand Hotel had. We drank and danced the night away.

A couple days later, they all flew back to the States. I planned to reconnect with Danny and Jackie once I was stateside to invite them to move up to North Carolina with Katrina and me. That way I would have someone there to watch the houses and take care of Katrina if she needed anything when I was away on business. This vacation had been a way to rekindle our friendship and see where everything stood. It seemed good and I was excited to get things rolling.

Things went well with the move. In just a short time we were moving to Robinsville, NC. Katrina and I rented a place on a mountain creek road. It was a newer two-bedroom, one-bathroom house and we were only the second tenants. It was a wood frame house with a fireplace in the living room. The kitchen was open to the living room with sliding glass doors off the side toward the road to a porch. Across the road was a creek that you could hear the water running in from the porch. The house was good and only Jackie and Danny plus their two young boys knew us. It all seemed like paradise.

Jackie and Danny had rented a house just a few miles away from us. Close enough but yet far enough away that we each had our own space. It was nice to have friends who already knew us so we wouldn't have to come up with a backstory. It was a place we could just be ourselves in.

It only took a couple months before someone contacted me to do another job. Katrina would stay in North Carolina snug, secure, and happy while I was away.

46

28' Broken Sailboat

Me, Mike, and two hired hands had a run set up to take a 28-foot sailboat to Nassau to pick up a load and sail back to Florida. Unfortunately it wasn't quite as simple as that.

The trip to Nassau was nothing out of the ordinary. It was a nice boat and after just a few hours on her I had a good feel for her. Only a mild breeze puffed the sails, so we spent the better part of two days getting to Nassau. On board we had close to a case of oil drums -- most were fake. They were the type that you stash things in. In our case, we were stashing rolls of hundred dollar bills. This was our traveling and buying cash.

After we had docked the boat and cleared customs in Nassau, it was time to get a meal and relax. I don't remember the name of the place we ate at but it was also a bar with plenty of music. When we finished eating, we just hung out and drank. Seems like places with music have a way of doing that to you: convincing you to just stay and hang out a little longer. As the night wore on, Mike got pretty buzzed. He had been sitting with some guy and his girlfriend or wife for quite some time now and I thought he was setting up a deal. Little did I know he was getting into trouble.

As the talk between Mike and the guy was getting louder and louder, I knew it was not a good sign. Their macho body language and pride-filled demeanor told me there was about to be trouble. I told the two guys with me to get out of the bar and stay out of sight. As the fight broke out, I went to Mike's aid. I did a bit of pushing and low gut punching so Mike could get away. I'll be damned if he didn't take advantage of the opportunity and took off leaving me holding the bag. I had only intended to help us both escape, not for him to run away and me to be stuck there fielding punches in the middle of a drunk brawl. The cops came, hauled me down to the police station, and threw me in a cell. The holding cell in Nassau was really small: about 5 feet wide and 7 feet long. There was a 2 foot wide by 30 inch high concrete bench on one side. The bathroom was a hole in the floor. It wouldn't have been quite so bad except there were six of us in the cell. The only good thing about it was no one talked to me. In return, I never said a word while in there.

The cops only held me until the people we'd had the problem with were off the island and on their way home. I was let out mid-morning the next day. I didn't get any food or water in lock-up, so as soon as they let me out, I walked right over to their water cooler and drank my fill. I believe that sure pissed them off. All of a sudden these two very large cops grabbed me up and put me in the backseat of a car with one of them on each side of me. As they were taking me to my sailboat to kick me off the island, they made it clear I was to leave as quickly as I could. They were leaning in on me, squishing me, trying to pull off the tough cop effect. I didn't say too much except I asked them how they knew I was on a sailboat. At least they gave me an honest answer. They responded that the two guys who had come with Mike and me had told the cops everything. So much for keeping a low profile.

After they dropped me off at the boat, I did a quick check of the oilcans. There wasn't a bill left in any of them. That wasn't a good sign. Shortly after I was on board, our two hired snitches showed up. That's when I found out that Mike had run to the airport and flown back to the States while I was locked up in jail. That SOB. He must've taken the money and run because neither one of our two goons had known anything about it.

There was nothing for me to do now but take the boat back to the States. The two that brought me back to the boat made it clear that they would be keeping an eye on me until I was well on my way. I tried to start the little onboard diesel so I would be able to navigate easily out of the harbor to the open water, but it wouldn't start. I opened the door to the engine to give it a look and the fuel line was unhooked. I went to put it back on and the fitting on the intake for the fuel had been removed! Now I was a little on edge. Here I was with two dummies who had told the cops too much. Mike was long gone safe, sound, and secure. The local cops were sitting there telling me to get the hell out, and someone had been messing with the onboard motor.

I ended up sailing the 28-footer out of Nassau and Paradise Island Harbor. I got real lucky and caught just enough wind to get through the harbor to open water. Once we were in open water, I set a course for North by Northwest heading for Grand Bahama Island just to have a landmark to sail towards in case of emergency. Before we took off, I had asked the cops in Nassau if I could pull into Grand Bahama. Their answer was a resounding "NO!" The next place for me to dock was the USA. And that would take some time since the wind was so low and not blowing a favorable direction.

The sailing was slow and the sun was hot. This gave me

plenty of time to talk to the two other guys on the boat. After a while they told me that the cops had questioned them and they had reported they didn't know anything. They claimed they were just along for the ride and that Mike and I were the main guys. Then they shared some real interesting information. They saw the police talking with Mike too. Mike had told the guys to hang out to see if I got out of jail and call him if I did. Mike especially wanted to be kept informed if the cops were going to take the boat. He told them if I didn't get out and they didn't take the boat, he would come back and sail it home. On the other hand, if the Nassau authorities did keep the boat and me, he would fly them home at least.

After listening to this I was none too pleased. Mike was such a double-crosser. There I was with two snitches on board with me and Mike the gutless coward that started the whole damn mess ran home. As I sat in the heat thinking of all the things I would like to do to all three of them, my crewmates gave me the idea for my next move.

They were talking about how they would like to cool off. So I suggested they get in the dinghy we were towing and I would use a bucket to get some water and throw over them. They didn't want to try to swim because we were under sail so couldn't possibly keep up with the boat. So after a while, we pulled the dinghy up close to the stern and they both got in. As I let the rope out, I took the bucket that was tied to a line and drop it overboard to get some water and threw it on them.

Now I had these two dumbasses where I wanted them. You see, this rubber raft didn't have a motor on it, and the oars were on board with me. I began to list to them all that they had done wrong. At first they back talked to me a little. So, I untied the rope to the dinghy and let it go. Within a moment they realized there was no land in sight.

They had no water to drink and no shade, not even a hat. They were in shorts only.

That was the moment their wrongs dawned on them. They were talking fast as I was being blown away. After I got a little ways off from them, they quit begging me to come back. I figured they had gotten the point, so I started to tack back to them. The wind was a beast to fight, so it took me most of an hour to retrieve them.

After they were on board and the dinghy was tied on again trailing nicely behind, there was no conversation. I could tell the boys were scared to death. They weren't sure what I would do next. For the next few hours they hardly moved. For sure they were not going to separate or take their eyes off of me.

As we were slowly moving toward the Grand Bahamas, a Coast Guard Learjet buzzed us, just checking on our movement. This made the two with me even more nervous. The Coast Guard had already been tipped off by the Nassau authorities that we were on a busted drug run, and all three of us in the boat knew who was responsible for spilling the beans. I kept them nervous all the way to where I anchored for the night on the lee side of Grand Bahama Island.

Now came a choice for my two now very worried passengers. I purposely brought the boat close to a sand bar not far off the island. If they decided to leave, it was an easy 100-foot swim to shallow water. I pretty much told them how far across the Gulfstream it was and you never could trust the weather. After my talk, they both jumped into the water and started swimming for the shallows. I was good with that. I didn't like them on board with me anyway. I never seen or heard from them ever again.

The rest of the sail back to the mainland was a good opportunity for me to air my head out and get over being mad about the whole trip. I was able to let it all go on the ocean waves: Mike, who blew the trip, started a fight in a bar, sabotaged the motor, took all the money, and the two morons that I just dumped. To get my sanity back, I started fishing.

I suppose I was moving around 6 knots give or take. So slow I just tied the tiller and baited a poll with a florescent yellow-green rubber squid. I dropped it off the back and let her out a good ways. I could see it every now and then bouncing on the waves. Then I stepped back to my spot to hold the tiller and watch the compass.

After a long spell, the reel started to sing. I had a strike, fish on! I threw the rope I had rigged as an autopilot over the tiller and jumped up to grab the rod. As I grabbed it and hit the tension lock to set the hook, it was thrilling. I could tell I had a good fish by the fight it was giving me. Then all at once it broke water and up in the air it flew. It was a beautiful sailfish. Now I was excited. I had never caught a fish like that before. I could not believe I caught it trawling on a sailboat on a botched job.

It must've taken 20 or 30 minutes to get the fish on board. There I was with a 4-foot sailfish and no one to see it. Of course I didn't have a camera, I was on a smuggling run. The only thing left to do was put the fish back in the water and hold it by the bill until it jerked out of my hand and was gone.

One good thing about catching that fish was it sure made the rest of the trip to West Palm Beach seem easy. Or at least the open sea part. Sailing through the inlet and down the intercostal was tough. I felt like I needed 4 hands or at least a trawling motor. By the time I got to the dock on the canal I was feeling pretty good about my sailing abilities.

When I stepped off the boat for the first time in a bit over four days, I had the overwhelming urge to find Mike and give him a beating.

But I suppose he knew I would feel that way because he was nowhere to be found. So I headed home. I needed a bath and some sleep pretty bad by then.

47
The 25' Mako's Extra Fuel Tank

Don and I had picked up a 25-foot Mako open fisherman. We had rigged her with gill brackets and two 235 Mercury outboard motors. I had been making runs back and forth to Grand Bahama island in her. They were mostly short hops because with the longer ones I had to stop too often for fuel. Don and I had talked about putting a long-range fuel tank inside the center console of the Mako so I'd be able to make longer runs and on a perfect run not have to stop for fuel at all. In theory it was a very good idea.

Meanwhile, Katrina and I were still living up in North Carolina just outside of Robbinsville. We were still renting a cabin on the side of a mountain using aliases of course. It was good there. Nobody seemed to ask any questions or have any suspicions.

While I was up in the mountains with Katrina and in between runs, Don and a couple other guys removed the center console on the Mako and came up with the measurements for an extra fuel tank. They built it out of plywood and some type of fiberglass that was supposed to be fuel resistant. The tank was large and would hold over 200 gallons of fuel with a pump system set up for when the standard tank got low. This would be the backup.

When we got ready to make another run, we filled the spare tank along with the standard tank. We needed to know how the extra weight was going to act at sea. As we were crossing, all seemed to be working fine. Since we had not set up for a quick turnaround, we would have to dock at Lucaya Harbor for at least one night to get a load set to go.

We pulled into the harbor late into the night. The dock master had already left so I found an empty slip and put the Mako in its place for the night. Now that we were done for the night, my mate and I decided to eat our dinner of cheese and grapes: two foods that always keep well on board without ice. After eating, we piled the seat cushions on top of the coolers and sleep came quickly after such a rigorous day at sea.

Just as dawn was breaking, I rolled over and put my feet down on the deck. That's when I noticed I was ankle-deep in what I thought was water. My first instinct was to hit the bilge pump switch thinking I must've left it in the "off" position instead of auto. Just as I hit the "on" switch, I realized how very cold the water was on my feet. As I came to a bit more, the smell of gas filled my nostrils. At that moment I realized I was standing in about 4 inches of gas! I froze and called my first mate to wake him up. I talked real slowly to him about not putting his feet down on the deck and that I was standing in gas. When he grasped the danger of the moment, he froze too.

We both knew we were in a heck of a spot. I instructed him to ease off the bow being especially careful not to rock the boat. The slightest spark or friction could send us booming in an instant. Meanwhile, the bilge pump I had switched on was pumping gas out of the boat into the harbor. It was a recipe for disaster and not looking good for me at all. After my mate was off the boat, I asked him to get a water hose from the dock and hook it to the nearest water supply.

This probably only took a few minutes, but standing in a death trap, it seemed like forever. By the time he got the hose hooked up, I had slowly moved to the bow of the boat. He handed me the hose so I could water down the fuel and keep the bilge pump underwater until the fumes from the gas were gone. The Mako is a self-bailing boat, so it was just a matter of waiting for the fluid to move off the deck. We had lots of fluid coming on and lots pumping out.

By the time we got things well under control, people were coming to life around the dock. We were lucky in many ways that morning. Right off, the boat should've exploded when I turned the bilge pump on while half asleep! Next thing was it was early and no one was awake on the dock but us. That in itself was almost unheard of. Because no one was awake, there were no cigarettes being thrown into the water or even being lit for that matter – another rarity amongst sailors! Also, there weren't any early-morning fisherman starting engines with 200 gallon of gas floating on the water. Oh yes, and then there was the fact, not the least of which, was that the catastrophe was at the hands of two smugglers that came into harbor in the cover of dark and hadn't cleared customs. Or for that matter, that no dock master or anyone else that may have seen the fuel spill notified police and fire department.

As the two of us were leaving the dock, I did hear a couple of people say something about smelling gas. So we beat feet to the store, bought a bottle of dishwashing soap and went to work scrubbing our shoes, our clothes, and ourselves at the pool shower by the Shalimar Hotel. When we went back to the boat, we washed it from bow to stern to get rid of the smell of fuel. Finally things were back to normal with an extra sparkle about them, I might add.

The easy part of that trip was buying some kilos of cocaine and smuggling them back to the States.

48

When the Boat Came Apart

It was summer and seas were calm on the way to Lucaya Harbor on Grand Bahama. My first mate and I had set off on yet another smuggling run for a few kilos of cocaine. The ride there was uneventful. Remember the gill brackets with the twin 235 engines on the back of the Mako? These brackets helped extend the length of the boat and gave me more control in heavy seas. Even though it was an older boat, and I had put many trips on it, she seemed good and solid.

After we got the boat docked at Lucaya Harbor, I spoke to the dock master. He already knew me from previous trips. I checked through customs with him using a fake name with a Florida driver's license and a birth certificate. I paid him a fee and that was it. He would watch my boat and he was covered because he had a name to go with the boat.

The first mate and I checked into the Shalimar Hotel. It wasn't real fancy, but still hosted a lot of tourists and other sailors, so we fit right in. After we were settled in the room, I told the mate to hang close to the hotel while I set things up. I was leaving all the buy money in the closet in the room, so it was his job to make sure it stayed nice and secure. We had a room with a view of the pool and the pool bar so he could keep our room in sight while sitting at the pool bar. I didn't want him holed up in the room as that would be suspicious in this vacation hotspot. No one goes there to sit in a hotel room and lurk over a pool and bar where everyone else is having a good time.

After I had set up the buy it was time to go get the money and take a boat ride to an outer island. This was a normal process so there was no worry. I would blend in with a couple of local fishermen. As we made our way out to open sea through a series of canals, we didn't draw any attention. Making our way to the small island to finalize the deal brought back memories of a time before and what I had found out there.

Richie, Wayne, Mike, Tuna, me, and a guy I'll just call Joe used to do a lot of work together in the drug smuggling business throughout the Caribbean. Joe had made some good money, about $25,000, and bought himself a boat and went to make a buy alone. He didn't tell us about this, we only found out when we were setting up a deal and called his wife but she said she thought he was already out on a trip already.

A few months passed and Mike and I were out doing a buy alongside the same island I was approaching now. We saw a boat moored in the lagoon. We knew the boat. It was Joe's boat. This area was well known for pirates, so it was another reason to never be in this kind of business alone. We didn't want to attract any attention to ourselves in case he was dealing with some trouble, so we did our deal and left.

A bit later that season, we had three boats all loaded to the gunwales with pot. A storm had come in and we needed to get some of the weight out of our boats or we might sink. We were close to the deal island once again, so we pulled in to a cove out of sight. We found a half-covered cave on the island so thought it was an ideal place to unload some of our pot to retrieve later. I remember the clouds were so gloomy and thick that it felt like nighttime even though it was actually mid-afternoon.

When we reached our destination with our partial loads, we unloaded and made some arrangements. The next day was bright and sunny, so we took two of the boats back to pick up the rest of our pot. As we cleared the cave, we looked around a little extra to make sure we didn't leave anything behind, then scoped out the area around the cave to look for any traces of exposure. We wanted to make sure we hadn't been seen. After all, this was not friendly territory.

That's when we found Joe's bones: in the bushes outside the cave. He must've had his money hidden as it appeared that whoever was after it had cut his hand off probably to make him talk. All that was left was a pile of bones and rags that had been his clothes. Needless to say, we got the hell out of there. We talked about telling his wife, but decided against it. We never saw or spoke to her again.

That's why dealing around that island always made me a little leery and put me on edge. But, we got in and made our buy without any problem. Once we got back to the boat and cleared the island, we put on our fishing act since that was our best cover for the area. Then we just stayed out real deep so no one would know if we were fishing or not. When we got back to Grand Bahama the next day we put the fishing boat away just like you would after fishing except the coolers we carried to the house didn't have fish in them. They were full of cocaine. Things had changed from pot to cocaine nowadays. It was the days of the Cocaine Cowboys. All about supplying the demand.

We set the spot I would bring the Mako around to where I would take on the load. One of the guys from the house would be sitting on the rocks fishing so he could hand me the coolers and we would be off. I went back to the hotel and got cleaned up so I didn't look like I had been up all night. I got the first mate and we grabbed some waters and beers, paid the hotel bill, and headed for the boat. We fueled the boat, paid for it, and tipped the dock master once again before we were off. He would log us out as if we had never been there so we'd leave no paper trail.

We met our fisherman and got our load on board. Even though we were on the lee side of the island it was pretty choppy. I had to stay on the wheel with one motor engaged to stay off the rocks while my mate and the fisherman got two coolers on board. Then we were off. Now that we were loaded and headed home, things were supposed to go smooth for the next couple of hours. Wrong!

As we came around the west end of Grand Bahama, the water was rough – something like 3- to 5-footers. Now these beat us up pretty good. When we got to the Gulfstream they got bigger, more like 5- to 7-feet. After taking a sound beating for almost an hour, things got worse. I kept watching the stern as some water was washing over the back. The more I watched the stern, the more it looked to me like it was moving separate from the boat. I was in disbelief though – how could that be? I asked my first mate to take the wheel while I went to take a look.

It was not good! Sure enough, the transit was breaking away from the boat. While the first mate was watching the helm and the compass heading, I took out some rope. I ran the rope from the side cleats back to where you would tie a ski rope on the outside of the transit. I doubled the line and pulled it tight. Then I took a short bar and started twisting a rope to tighten it as tight as I could. After twisting both sides tight, I could still see movement. But it was down to under a half inch. That was an improvement at least since it had started at well over an inch.

I went back to take the wheel from my mate and told him it wasn't looking good. I asked him to get each of us a life jacket. After we had those on I told him to take the rest of the lifejackets and tie them to the to Igloo coolers and lash them together and set them out in the open so they'd pop up easily in case the boat capsized. With that done, I did the only thing left to do. I had my mate grab us some beers and sit tight on the rocket launcher seat. It was time to relax and not look back anymore. I sat the throttle at 2600 RPM for each of the engines and headed west. We were too far out into the Gulfstream to retreat.

Slowly, we churned toward West Palm Beach. At about the three-hour mark we could see the three stacks at the old power plant. I'd had a lot of close calls, but I was pretty excited that time around to see those smokestacks. We limped the boat all the way past peanut island and up onto the bow trailer. I believe we forgot about the load we were hauling since it was still sitting out in the open for all to see. We were just so happy to have made it across for the last time in the Mako.

Since the Mako had to be retired, it was time to get a new boat. After some shopping, we acquired a 30-foot Scarab. It was an open fisherman type and we rigged it with two Johnson motors. It was a smooth running boat, but a bit on the wet side as most scarabs are. I made quite a few runs in this boat and she had proved solid and stalwart, so we decided that there should be two of them in our little drug fleet. We would leave both boats identical: unnamed, undistinguishable, and perfect for playing into our hand. The plan was that if anyone was watching the inlet and saw a boat go out and than saw the same boat come back in there would be less of a chance that they would stop and board the boat. Even if they were watching for smugglers.

49
Last Trip

I was back at home in North Carolina in the cabin that Katrina and I were living in on the side of the mountain. Our low-profile move was turning out real nice for us. Katrina had Danny and Jackie to keep her company and it was a good setup for us all. This was always my base I'd run back to between smuggling trips and in the off-season. Life was good.

I got a call from Don one day that it was time to make another run. I started to make the usual preparations. I tried to get a hold of my regular first mate but I had no luck whatsoever. He didn't answer his phone or any of the messages I left him.

Time was running low and I needed another guy on this trip. This put me in a bind and I made a bad call. I broke one of my own rules and asked Danny to go with me. You see, Danny was my ex-wife's sister's husband. My rule was that you NEVER take family on a job. But at that moment, I didn't think there would be a problem because I had made many smooth runs up to now so I asked Danny if he wanted to make $10,000 and I'd throw in a new car for Jackie. He was more than happy with the offer and I had my first mate. We packed a small bag each and hit the road south.

    We met up with Don in Bradenton, Florida where we picked up the 30-foot Scarab. I did a once over to make sure the boat was ready to run. After everything checked out, we got some rest at a motel on the outskirts of Riviera Beach. The next morning we set the boat to water like we were going fishing. Don backed us into the water from the ramp and took care of hiding the truck and trailer. He was supposed to put together our second 30-foot scarab that would match the one I was running so that when I was coming back he would launch the other scarab and go out leaving me free to come in and unload our goods into the trailer. Once the smuggling boat was loaded and clear, we'd come back and pick up Don and the second boat. It was a very simple clean plan for this side of the water.

    Danny and I had a smooth trip to Grand Bahama. I briefed Danny about some of how the plan would work. Nothing serious, just where we would be staying and some do's and don'ts to keep a low profile. I gave him his new identification papers and told him to stash his real ID in a waterproof bag that we would hide on the boat. The ID change was what we always did. There was no reason for anyone to know our real names, even if my real one was just another fake one. But Danny had only been Danny his whole life.

    It was odd I suppose as I think back to it, but none of the people who knew me in those days had any idea who I really was. Danny for instance didn't even know my real name. Just Rowdy. I suspect that at some point Danny might have known the name William Van Sant was associated with me, but I am not 100 percent of that because he didn't tell people who would interrogate him later. As for most other people, they just never asked for a name other than Rowdy. They all knew me so well and really didn't even know me at the same time.

Quite an irony. I had told some of them that I was on the lam, and what they knew of me was not really me. Most of them thought I was lying to them. How little they really knew.

We arrived at the dock at Lucaya Harbor with no problem. Just like the dozens of previous runs I had done, we were set with the boat tied, customs cleared, dock master paid. Now to check into the good old Shalimar Hotel. It had everything we'd need, so I left Danny there and took care of the real deal.

I got a hold of my connection and I told him what I needed. By this time he was more of a friend than anything else. I brought him a new Browning 9 mm pistol for a gift. He tried to get me to come work for him as his personal boat captain. He told me he was in the process of buying the boat that won the Nassau to Miami race the year before and wanted me to run it. It was an appealing offer. I decided to think it over, but for now I was already tied up in the deal that we were doing.

It took almost 4 days to get the load ready. I was not the only buyer that was there at the time. There were enough of us that a trip had to be made to Columbia. The plane left the first day I arrived, but the weather held it down for two days in Columbia. Then as soon as it landed we would want to load and head out. The more you hang around, the more obvious you became. Not a good practice in our business.

The plane landed early in the evening so we planned to pull out the next day. As soon as it landed I went to the hotel to get Danny so we could prep and fuel the boat like we were going fishing in the morning. We got the cooler and brought it back to our hotel room so we could top it off from the hotel's ice machine before we left in the morning. You always have to keep a cooler so you can have water and other drinks to take on the trip. You never go to sea without preparing to be stranded out there – I had sure learned that lesson! If you do happen to sink your boat, coolers float so you can survive. Amazing the multi-purpose powers of these Styrofoam containers!

After prepping the boat, Danny went back to the hotel and I went to see the Old Man where I looked the merchandise over and packed it in a duffel bag to be ready for morning.

We were up and at the dock just before dawn. I paid off the dock master and he gave me the customs papers so it would never show us even being there. Then we were off. We were to make the hand-off from shore to boat in a rocky cove west of Lucaya. The Old Man would be there to make sure the it went well.. As I held the boat just off the edge of the rocks, Danny went forward and got the bag from the drop man. Then there was a wave to the Old Man and I backed away from the rocks and set out for home.

The ride back toward Palm Beach was a smooth one. There were only swells way apart creating a smooth roll. I set the RPMs on the engines and adjusted the trim tabs and set back to drink a cold beer. Coming back is always what got my adrenaline pumping. I believe that's the part I liked most about smuggling. It put me back on point, back on the edge. I got hooked on this feeling back in Vietnam and hadn't been able to leave the edge alone ever since. Some call it an effect of PTSD. For me, between the recurring nightmares and adrenaline rushes, I was right at home. Hell, if I wasn't in a shoot out every six months or so, I would start to worry that it was my time and I just couldn't see it coming.

We made it across the Gulfstream in about two hours so we were just hanging out offshore waiting to see our matching boat come out of the inlet so we could head in. I had sent the message ahead that I'd be going fishing that day which was Don's signal. When there was no sign of our twin by 10 am, all kinds of things started to run through my mind. Maybe they broke down or the boat wasn't ready or 10 dozen other things. I decided we couldn't wait any longer, so I started in. Little did I know these were the last few hours I would be free for the next few years.

As we came through the inlet by peanut island all was well. After we cleared the inlet into the intercostal, a Marine patrol boat moved into the inlet behind us to block it. I looked toward the West and a helicopter popped up into view. At that moment, I knew we were in a bad spot. I told Danny to throw away the fake ID I had given him as I was ripping mine apart simultaneously. I made him change shirts with me real fast in case we'd been spotted by someone. My mind was racing with any precaution we needed to take to lessen the heap of trouble we were in. I was in survival mode and now it was how I could keep Danny clear since I had gotten him in this.

With no way out, we were getting close to the bridge by the dock. I told Danny to start cutting the kilos and throwing them out in the water. The saltwater would dissolve the cocaine and they'd have nothing on us. As we went under the bridge, I knew everything was wrong. Raymond Parker was under the bridge waving at me. This was not the plan, I didn't even like that asshole and sure as ever didn't trust him. I'd soon find out why.

Later I learned that Raymond Parker was there and not Don because they had done a deal with some guys they didn't know from the Florida Panhandle who turned out to be undercover cops. Then they had ratted me out since I was the bigger fish to the cops, and to the Feds. Raymond Parker had been sent to set me up. The whole situation still makes me mad enough to spit fire.

Danny tossed the duffel bag overboard as we passed under

the bridge. The only problem was that it wasn't empty, is still had 3 keys in it, and he hadn't slashed those bags so the saltwater could dissolve it. I didn't know that at the moment, nor did I know that he hadn't listened to me and destroyed his fake ID. That all came to light later.

Now that we were past the bridge, I swung the boat around the island to the dock at a speed well above no wake. When we hit the dock, I jumped off the boat followed closely by Danny. We didn't bother to shut her off, we knew we were in trouble so we just headed for my truck. The truck wasn't even hooked to the trailer, which was all wrong of course, but at the moment it was good for me.

Thank goodness I always carried a spare key to the truck so we were off in a matter of seconds. As I cranked it up, cops, mostly plainclothes type came in on us from every direction. It didn't matter to me as the truck was running and it was a four-wheel drive. I dropped her into drive and I was off. The chase was on, I ended up on PGA Boulevard running lights and passing everything in sight. I had a line of cop cars with lights flashing and sirens blaring trailing us. There were two helicopters, one to my left and the other to the right behind us. I knew we were short-lived for this ride, so I started giving Danny the down low. I told him not to say anything. They didn't have any 8 x 10 glossies of us (which was the photographic proof they would need), all the kilos were gone, and all they were going to find on the boat was a waterproof bag, some money, and IDs.

Danny had hardly said a word since we had passed into the inlet. I knew he was scared to death. All I could hope was that he would remember what I had said about their lack of proof. They had nothing solid, so as long as he didn't say anything, we'd both be out by morning.

I still had my foot floored on the gas pedal as I was flying west on PGA Boulevard. We had made it a little over 20 blocks when we came over a small rise in the road to see a wall of cop cars. They were ready for us, out of their cars and all guns drawn. I slammed on the brakes and came to a stop within 10 feet of the blockade. Within just a few moments, they had us out of the truck and up against the side of it. A few of them were talking smack to us, but neither of us said anything.

They separated us at that point and took us to the DEA building in downtown West Palm Beach. We were on the tenth floor and of course they were trying to get us to talk. Talk about what I'm not sure. Little did I know that Danny was in another room telling everything he could think of. The DEA had told him how he would never see his wife or kids again as a free man if he didn't talk. He talked so much that they had to slap him so he would shut up long enough to turn the tape over. Danny told them everything he knew about me from the first day he met me. I guess that's what I get for breaking my own rule about family. I can't blame him though. Danny wasn't really cut out for this line of work. I had roped him into it out of desperation. Of course I just had to pick the one guy who was least prepared for this kind of trouble the moment I was getting set up.

After they got what they wanted from Danny and knowing they had Raymond Parker and Don all wrapped up, they came to pressure me. Danny had told them about the fake IDs and of course handed his over since he'd kept it like an idiot. They wanted mine too, but that was impossible since it was gone. They also told me they had retrieved 3 kg in the duffel bag. I just acted like I didn't even know what they were talking about. After about an hour or so, I got tired of them playing games with me. They thought they were so damn smart. The truth is, they only knew what some snitch told them – though I didn't say that to them at that point. But I'm sure they knew it. They couldn't do their own detective work, it was all about getting the dirt from other sources after they'd pressured them into losing everything they had. I was sick of it all, so I said, "If you're going to take me to jail, just do it." And that pissed them off enough so that's just what they did. I was off to MCC Miami for a federal vacation.

What happened after this is a tale of its own with life in Federal Prison and a judge to change my name again. After all the times I had changed my name to keep clear of going to prison, it felt a bit odd when, after 7 years 9 months and 27 days in prison, they would not let me out until they changed my name.

Starting over and being forced to go straight would test my metal to a whole other degree. Time to start over, but this time I would have to play by the rules. No fabricated background, no juggling fake names, no cutting deals and gun slinging, no serving my own justice, no flying under the radar, no skipping the country, no fun. I would be forced to deal with life on "Special" Parole. That meant getting a real job on the legal side of things. Because I was being watched like a hawk, I would no longer have the option to slink back to the under world culture that I lived in and had known so well before.

Adapting to life in the real world wasn't something I felt too confident about, especially with my PTSD issues. At least prison had given me some more clues and coping mechanisms to better deal with that. But really, there was just too much of my old lifestyle in me for it not to still affect everything that I would do moving forward.

Overshadowing all the issues I still had was the one big problem that chewed at me more than anything else: how would I find Katrina?

Rowdy Gifford was raised a Midwest farm boy and served in the Vietnam War from 1970 thru 1971.

A true jack-of-all-trades, he has mastered several skills from plumbing and gardening to body building and baking. Since coming clean from drug running, dealing & importing, and a recovered AA, he writes to keep his PTSD at bay and stay focused on leading a productive lifestyle.

He enjoys volunteering in the community and riding his motorcycle. Rowdy lives in Davie, FL with his wife Katrina and their dog Mr. Bo Jangles.